# PLASTiKi

# PLASTIKI

## ACROSS THE PACIFIC ON PLASTIC: AN ADVENTURE TO SAVE OUR OCEANS

### DAVID DE ROTHSCHILD

AS TOLD TO JIM GORMAN

FOREWORD BY ACHIM STEINER

EXECUTIVE DIRECTOR, U.N. ENVIRONMENT PROGRAMME

PUBLISHED BY

CHRONICLE BOOKS
San Francisco

PRODUCED BY

MELCHER MEDIA

Library of Congress Cataloging-in-Publication Data:
Rothschild, David de.
 Plastiki : across the Pacific on plastic, an adventure to save our oceans / by David
de Rothschild, as told to Jim Gorman  ; foreword by Achim Steiner.
    p. cm.
 ISBN 978-1-4521-0002-9
1.  Pacific Ocean--Description and travel. 2.  Pacific Ocean--Environmental
conditions. 3.  Plastiki (Boat) 4.  Marine resources conservation--Pacific Ocean.
I. Gorman, James, 1949- II. Title.
 G477.R68 2011
 910.9164--dc22
                        2010043046

Manufactured in China

Produced by Melcher Media
124 West 13th Street
New York, New York 10011
www.melcher.com

10 9 8 7 6 5 4 3 2 1

CHRONICLE BOOKS

680 Second Street
San Francisco, California 94107
www.chroniclebooks.com

To my family, loved ones, and team, without whom I am nothing. And to those who believed in
the dream, took the pledge, and doubted we could ever make it! Sail on.
— David de Rothschild

# TABLE OF CONTENTS

# FOREWORD

Achim Steiner, UN Under-Secretary General and Executive Director,
UN Environment Programme (UNEP)

The genesis and journey of *Plastiki* and its courageous crew will surely enter the annals of maritime history as one of courage and determination.

Sailing a catamaran 8,000 nautical miles across the Pacific is no mean feat—but to do it floating on 12,500 plastic bottles glued together with adhesives derived from sugar and cashew nuts makes the voyage doubly remarkable.

But without a doubt, David de Rothschild and his team's lasting legacy will be the global attention they have put on the menace to the world's seas and oceans from humanity's currently wasteful ways.

Despite some successes, such as a decline in radioactive materials and persistent organic pollutants in parts of the Atlantic, the marine environment continues to be all too often treated as a dustbin.

*Plastiki* has highlighted the threats from plastics, perhaps the most visible symbol of this unsustainable past and ongoing present.

The North Pacific gyre concentrates 3.5 million tons of discarded plastic—one of five such swirling waste patches in the world.

*Plastiki* has helped to focus the minds of a global public on the way contemporary economies all too often squander and mismanage finite and fragile natural resources.

There is, however, another side to the *Plastiki* story: the change possible through human ingenuity, resourcefulness, and ambition to meet challenges head on.

We are delighted to have been involved in this remarkable story. It was, in David's own words, inspired by a UNEP report on marine litter from 2006—living proof that United Nations reports can make a difference.

A staff member was present at the launch in San Francisco and again as the catamaran entered Sydney harbor in triumph with UNEP's blue flag fluttering from the foremast.

I and many other staff members were also there in spirit through the crew's blogs, which were often gripping and witty—essential daily reading. *Plastiki* has delivered a metaphorical message in a bottle to millions upon millions of people.

UNEP will also be there in the future, supporting *Plastiki*'s extraordinary legacy, taking forward our ongoing work assessing trends in the marine environment, and assisting governments toward the actions so urgently needed.

# 1

AN EPIPHANY—"LET'S BUILD A BOAT OUT OF PLASTIC BOTTLES AND SAIL ACROSS THE PACIFIC"—BECOMES A MISSION, A MESSAGE, AND AN EXPEDITION.

OUT OF THE DARKNESS, A GIFT. OF SORTS. A BIG WET KISS FROM THE OCEAN PLANTED SQUARELY ON MY CHEEK. AND MY HEAD, AND THE REST OF ME. A TRICKLE OF ICY SEAWATER HAS SOMEHOW WORKED ITS WAY PAST MY FORTRESS OF GORE-TEX, DOWN THE NAPE OF MY NECK, AND EVER SO SKILLFULLY ALONG THE LENGTH OF MY SPINE INTO MY HERETOFORE WARM AND DRY LONG JOHNS.

I'm only thirty seconds into a three-hour tour of duty on watch, the tiller and beanbag chair still imprinted with our co-skipper Mr. T's warmth. Just over a week removed from a grand departure from San Francisco, and nothing yet about life at sea—the constant motion, the middle-of-the-night wake ups, the tiger-in-a-cage restlessness of living on a 20-by-60-foot platform with five other people—resembles comfortable routine.

"Did that one get you?" asks Mr. T with a grin. "Nice! Got off just in time." His silhouette dissolves quickly into the red glow of the cabin. Alone.

"Oh, yes! Wet again!" I yell into the night, the sound of my voice devoured by the blackness.

Really, Dave? Really? There isn't even a breath of wind or a ripple on the ocean, and you still find a way to get wet. I guess that's the true meaning of a rogue wave. A stream of phosphorescence pulsing and swirling on the port side catches my eye and distracts me from my situation.

And what a situation! What was I thinking in wanting to sail the entire Pacific Ocean? Can I legitimately use the word *thinking* in conjunction with building a boat from 12,500 plastic bottles and then attempting to sail from San Francisco to Sydney?

My eyes flicker back and forth trying to find some focus in the black void. Our boat is moving along at a speed of less than 2 knots, if you can call that moving. Bobbing is more like it. This is going to be a long journey, I fear.

"Hey, Mr. T! Do you think we'll make Sydney?"

"Not this year," comes the reply from out of the glowing cabin.

I'm sailing the dream: The *Plastiki,* after two years of hard work, is our best and most sincere expression of the fresh ideas necessary to create a better future. A future that avoids the unsustainable waste and environmental damage of our current way of living. A future that sees waste as a resource—like the 12,500 reused plastic bottles I'm floating on right now.

Yet tonight I can't stop thinking I've bitten off more than I can chew. Maybe the doubters and naysayers were right. Surely, just sailing across San Francisco Bay would

DAVID DE ROTHSCHILD STEERS *PLASTIKI* THROUGH ONE OF MANY INTENSE PACIFIC DOWNPOURS.

have proven my point. Be careful what you wish for, I always tell others. Maybe I need to start heeding my own advice.

• • •

Salt does not course through my veins. I know a jib from a mizzen, and a cleat from a winch, but the extent of my nautical experience prior to *Plastiki* amounted mostly to sailing Hobie Cats while on family vacations as a kid.

It wasn't salt water but ice that was the medium for my first big adventures. On ski expeditions across Antarctica, Greenland, and the Arctic, I logged hundreds of days and nights on frozen surfaces. While brutally cold and rife with dangers, polar environments in my estimation offer a distinct advantage over the open ocean: They tend not to pitch and roll beneath you. They're also impossibly pristine and beautiful and, as we're discovering in a warming world, quite fragile.

*Plastiki*'s journey began years before the boat ever touched water. In June 2006, I'd just returned to London from an expedition to cross over the North Pole from Russia to Canada. It had been humbling—rapidly melting pack ice had ended our journey two hundred miles short of Canada. I saw how one of the earth's ecosystems was changing right before my eyes. And while thousands of schoolkids around the world had joined the "Top of the World" journey via the Web, I wanted the expedition to do more than raise awareness. I wanted to make it personal, to make everyone feel connected to the earth's fragility.

After any expedition there is some readjustment. It's an anticlimax. You've been living closely with your teammates in some of the most extreme and inspiring natural environments and then, with the planting of a flag or the last stroke of a paddle, it's over. Back in the real world, the thought kept running through my mind: "What's next? What can I do to keep the momentum going?"

IN 2006, DAVID DE ROTHSCHILD CROSSED THE ARCTIC—WITH MORE THAN 1 MILLION FOLLOWERS ON THE ADVENTURE ECOLOGY WEBSITE.

THE GREAT PACIFIC GARBAGE PATCH, ONE OF FIVE
OCEAN GYRES THAT ACCUMULATE TINY BITS OF
PLASTICS AS WELL AS LARGER MARINE DEBRIS
AND OTHER TRASH, NOW EXTENDS OVER AN
AREA TWICE THE SIZE OF TEXAS.

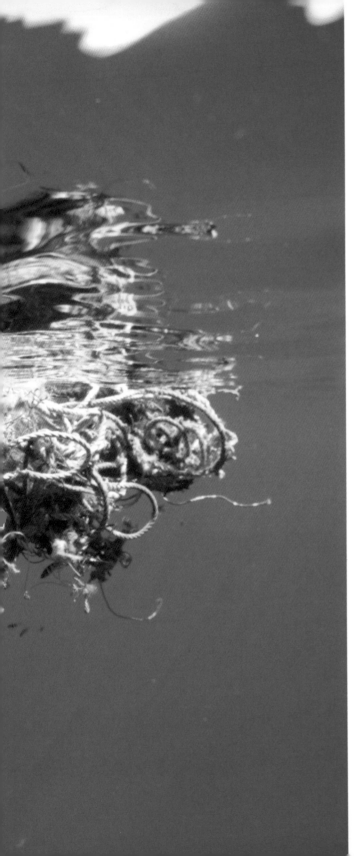

Whatever the next expedition turned out to be about, I was resolved that it had to move beyond simply raising awareness of an environmental problem. It needed to touch people's lives, it needed to provoke an emotional response, and it had to point the way toward solutions. I felt strongly on these counts. Here I was, only weeks removed from having spent one hundred days living on the ice, and already I was feeling disconnected from what had transpired in the Arctic. If I was feeling that way, then how could I expect other people to relate to my experience?

EVERY SQUARE MILE OF OCEAN CONTAINS 46,000 PIECES OF FLOATING PLASTIC GARBAGE. EVERY SQUARE MILE!

While researching potential themes for a new expedition, I stumbled upon a small passage in an obscure report issued by the United Nations Environment Programme (my reading interests can run a bit geeky) that opened my eyes to an issue I was unaware of. Buried within "Ecosystems and Biodiversity in Deep Waters and High Seas" was this astounding fact: Every square mile of ocean contains 46,000 pieces of floating plastic garbage. Every square mile! I thought that this must have been a typo. I even asked UNEP. Nope. The stat turned out to be correct. How could this be?

I dug deeper. From reports by Greenpeace and the Algalita Marine Research Foundation, I learned that the vast majority of marine waste is composed of plastic and, further, this pollution congregates in five enormous, slowly spinning ocean eddies. One estimate states that in the Eastern Garbage Patch, a gyre in the North Pacific that's approximately twice the size of Texas, every pound of plankton is outmatched by 6 pounds of plastic litter.

I went online to find out more about these garbage gyres. What was in them? Could you see them from space? What harm were they doing to marine life?

I couldn't find much of anything. Not in academic journals, not in the popular press. "Hang on a second," I thought. "This can't be true." Why doesn't everyone know that our oceans are filling up with trash? Here was this amazing, disgusting manifestation of modern waste and overconsumption floating ominously between Hawaii and California, and it was effectively a secret.

The thought of these human fingerprints smudging the oceans both alarmed and inspired me. What could I do to create an energy that would help solve this problem? From that question sprang the dream of *Plastiki*. The details would follow, but I knew then that I'd throw myself and the full resources and passions of the Adventure Ecology team, the expeditionary environmental organization I had launched in 2005 for the Arctic journey, into tackling marine debris.

· · ·

Plastic pollution is a massive and at the same time intensely personal environmental problem. Although the effects of global warming—caused by colorless, odorless gases—are not yet widely felt, we touch and see plastic every day of our lives. With every trip to the grocery store or takeout deli, we can readily see our waste footprint grow. On the bright side, all of us can do something immediate and measurable to reduce it.

A good starting point would be bottled water, which epitomizes the absurdity of our throwaway society. Each and every day, Americans consume 70 million bottles of water—nearly 9 billion gallons of bottled water a year. This despite the fact that the purity and taste of the water in those bottles is often lower than the water flowing freely from taps in our homes and workplaces. Only one in six plastic water bottles in the United States is recycled. The rest, some 22 *billion* empty plastic bot-

tles a year in the United States, end up in landfills and incinerators, or as trash in the street waiting for the next rainstorm to sweep them into our seas.

It was a few months later that I had what can only be described as an epiphany. I'd gone to Los Angeles in August 2006 to meet with Jeff Skoll, the first president at eBay and now chairman of Participant Media, the film production company behind *The Cove*; *Food, Inc.*; and *An Inconvenient Truth,* among other movies. I'd talked with Jeff about an idea for drawing attention to marine pollution: I'd take a bunch of artists out to the Eastern Garbage Patch and have them make sculptures of trash pulled from the ocean. The whole thing would be filmed documentary style. Jeff was unimpressed. "Where's the drama? What's the hook?" he asked. He was entirely right. The idea was flat.

I WENT ONLINE TO FIND OUT MORE ABOUT THESE GARBAGE GYRES. WHAT WAS IN THEM? COULD YOU SEE THEM FROM SPACE? WHAT HARM WERE THEY DOING TO MARINE LIFE?

Flying back to London, I could see the dazzling snows of the Arctic and then Greenland, sites of my previous adventures, slide past far below. Then came miles upon miles of blue ocean. My mind went back to Jeff's words. Where was the drama? I started to think about the big, game-changing expeditions of the past. When it comes to oceans, there is only one that comes to mind: the *Kon-Tiki.*

Who doesn't know of *Kon-Tiki*, the legendary balsa raft that Norwegian adventurer Thor Heyerdahl sailed from Peru to Polynesia in 1947? Heyerdahl and a crew of very game fellow Scandinavians lived out his theory of oceanic migration as they traveled the Pacific. I've always

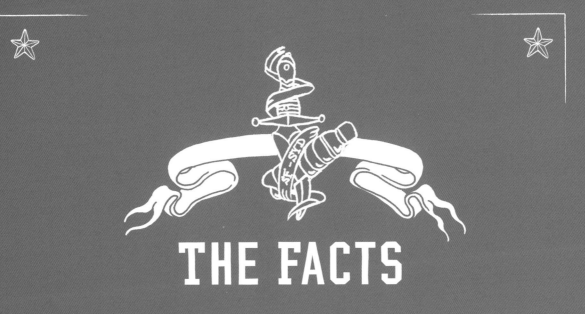

# THE FACTS

80 PERCENT OF OCEAN POLLUTION BEGINS ON LAND.

ALMOST 75 PERCENT OF THE WORLD'S FISH STOCKS
ARE ALREADY FISHED UP TO OR BEYOND
THEIR SUSTAINABLE LIMIT.

FOR EVERY 1 TON OF PLASTIC WE RECYCLE,
WE SAVE ALMOST 2,000 POUNDS OF OIL.

THE VOYAGE OF THE *KON-TIKI* IS ONE OF THE MOST COMPELLING ADVENTURES OF MODERN TIMES. THOR HEYERDAHL FOLLOWED HIS DREAM, AND THE WORLD HAS NEVER FORGOTTEN.

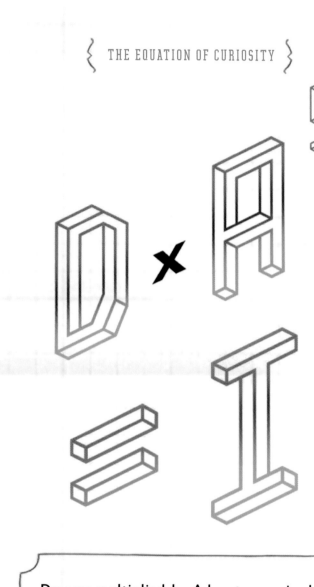

Dreams multiplied by Adventure, raised to the power of the Stories those adventures generate, produces Inspiration. The more dreams, the more inspiration—which leads to more dreams. It's a perpetual-motion machine—a philosophy rooted in mankind's irrepressible impulse to explore and then tell compelling stories about those adventures.

considered the voyage of the *Kon-Tiki* one of the most compelling and captivating adventures of modern times. Heyerdahl followed his dream, and the world has never forgotten.

"There it is," I practically shouted out on the plane. *Kon-Tiki. Plastiki.* If plastic was the main human fingerprint on the oceans, then why not use it as the basis for a craft, a boat that would highlight this mess. "Let's build a boat out of plastic bottles and sail across the Pacific." Now that would be dramatic. It would be more than a voyage across the ocean; the boat would prove the point that plastic didn't have to end up as waste, but that the material was misunderstood and misused.

At Adventure Ecology, I operate on a philosophy called the Equation of Curiosity: $D \times A^S = I$. Simply put, dreams are the breeding grounds for adventures; adventures spawn stories; and stories produce the inspiration needed to seed more dreams. The whole equation is driven by curiosity. It's a perpetual-motion machine—a philosophy rooted in mankind's, especially children's, ability to ask questions and to dream.

*Plastiki* would do homage to Heyerdahl and his brave team and, if we were lucky, bring ideas and ideals together much as *Kon-Tiki* did to create an epic adventure on the open sea. The adventure of *Plastiki*, from San Francisco to Sydney, would showcase a new way of thinking about waste, and it would generate the stories to inspire more new ways of thinking, more dreams, more adventures.

· · ·

We should have seen the tugboat bearing down on us, but we were absorbed by the task at hand: trying to fix our boat's broken steering mechanism. Somehow the bracket holding the tiller and rudder together had popped out. The horn blast caught our attention. Behind the tug came a barge piled high with coal bound for the docks in Oakland. Loads that large just don't turn

on a dime. Without steering and with the motor launch that had towed us out into San Francisco Bay fast disappearing, we were sitting ducks. Our Planet 2.0 solution was about to be undone by cold, hard Planet 1.0 reality. I could see the headlines, drenched in irony: CRAZY ENVIRO ON BOTTLE BOAT SMACKED TO DEATH BY COAL BARGE. Thanks to some spare rope and quick thinking, we lashed together the tiller and rudder and scooted out of the tug's path at the last second.

THE ADVENTURE OF PLASTIKI WOULD SHOWCASE A NEW WAY OF THINKING ABOUT WASTE, AND IT WOULD GENERATE THE STORIES TO INSPIRE MORE DREAMS.

Not every moment of *Plastiki*'s creation was that dramatic, although there were plenty of highs and more than a few lows. That day on the bay definitely ranked up there as a high, if you ignore the coal barge. The boat wasn't the 60-foot-long *Plastiki* but rather a 20-foot prototype built of marine plywood. The exciting discovery we made on that maiden voyage in June 2008—besides needing to strengthen the tiller-rudder bracket!—was that our concept of a boat made of bottles was viable. It floated. It sailed. The final *Plastiki* was still far off, more of a twinkle in our eyes at that juncture, but her pedigree was solid.

The first major step forward in moving *Plastiki* from dream to reality came when I met Michael Pawlyn in October 2007 at Google Zeitgeist, a conference of business and media leaders. Michael is a passionate advocate and practitioner of sustainable design inspired by nature, often called biomimicry. His architectural designs include several of the remarkable domed biomes at the United Kingdom's Eden Project and the fantastic

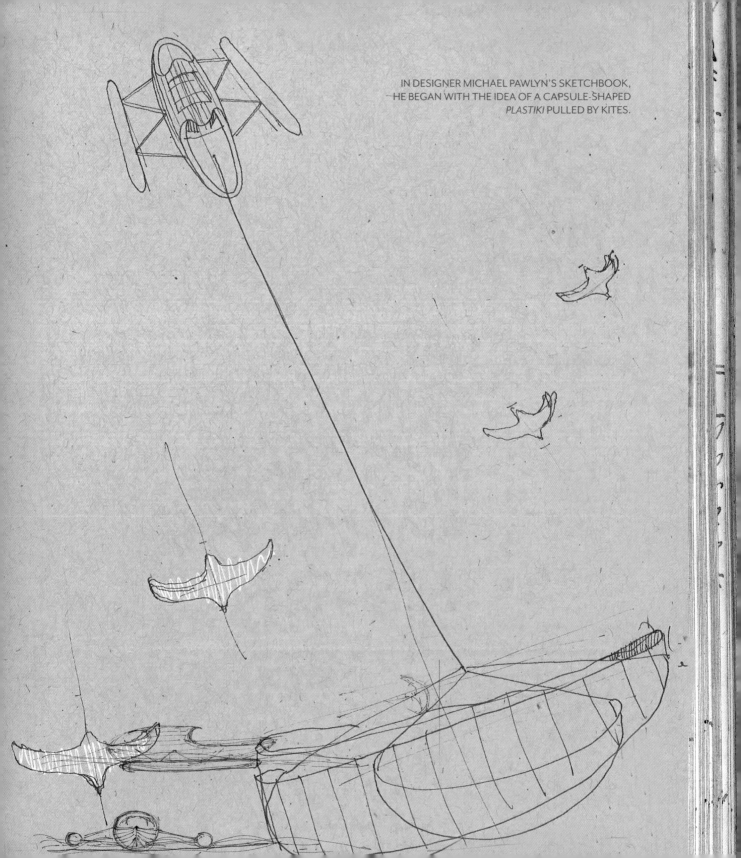

IN DESIGNER MICHAEL PAWLYN'S SKETCHBOOK, HE BEGAN WITH THE IDEA OF A CAPSULE-SHAPED *PLASTIKI* PULLED BY KITES.

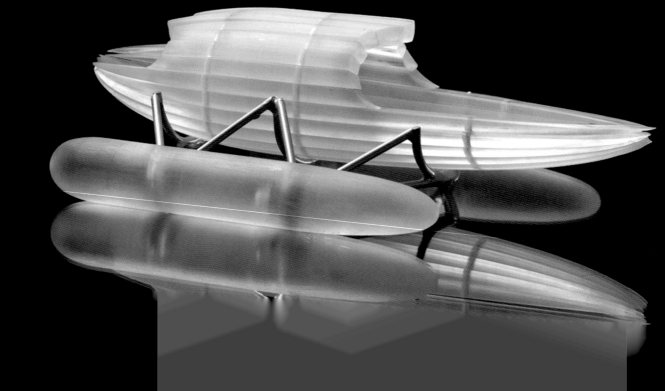

Las Palmas Water Theatre in the Canary Islands. "I really like what you're doing," I told Michael. "Rather than hire a naval architect, which I should probably do, I'd like to hire you instead." I wanted someone with no preconceived ideas about what a sailing vessel must be.

Michael didn't disappoint. I had only two requirements: The plastic bottles in our bottle boat had to be visible and functional. I had an open mind, but I guess I expected something like a raftlike platform floating atop big pouches of plastic bottles.

When the time came for Michael's first presentation, he arrived at Adventure Ecology's offices and set a box on the table. He lifted the lid and pulled out a model of a crazy-looking water bug. It looked like a trimaran, with two pontoons and a fuselage down the middle. Instead of using conventional sails, the boat's propulsion was to come by kite sail. The team was captivated.

The natural form that inspired Michael's solution for housing the soda bottles was the pomegranate. Within a pomegranate, the individual seeds are soft and easily crushed, but packed in pith and sheathed in a tough skin, the whole is very strong. In Michael's design, masses of tightly packed bottles, framed and skinned, would constitute the central hull and cabin as well as the two outrigger-style hulls. Bamboo and plywood would provide support and rigidity. During the ensuing give-and-take of the design process (and realities of building a craft that could sail 8,000 miles across the Pacific), we lost some elements of Michael's concept, but his biomimicry-based notion for integrating plastic bottles into *Plastiki*'s pontoons remained.

Finding someone who could translate Michael's concept into blueprints proved demanding. After fits and starts with architects who either couldn't grasp Michael's ideas and our intent, or who declined to participate due to the risks to the boat and their reputations, we lucked out in hiring Andy Dovell, a renowned Australian naval architect whose boats have competed in three America's Cups and numerous other sailing races. He's known for boats that are fast and elegant—and for liking a challenge. That last quality would serve him and the *Plastiki* team well in the months ahead. His first clue that this was no ordinary project came when he attended a design charrette at Adventure Ecology. We had convened a group of thirty people to kick around solutions to the problem of building a seaworthy boat out of an inherently weak material, and making it a floating "closed loop," capable of generating its own energy and water, and able to manage the crew's waste.

"IF WE CAN DESIGN OUR WAY INTO DIFFICULTY, WE CAN DESIGN OUR WAY OUT."—JOHN THACKARA
@DREXPLORE 5:32 A.M., JULY 17, 2009

Andy's initial design for *Plastiki* was a big departure from Michael's concept. We had become very attached to the initial designs, but Andy said we couldn't go forward as planned. The boat would twist and break apart under the incredible multidirectional forces the ocean would throw our way. As a future crew member, I thought these concerns seemed valid! Andy made it clear that we needed more stiffness to the structure, that we had to create a superstructure to hold the bottles. The initial design he came up with that day is almost 100 percent identical to the 60-foot catamaran that eventually sailed the Pacific. Looking back, it's apparent that Andy is a genius—one of the most talented people I might ever work with.

Now we had a new challenge, one that would take

# CREW PROFILE: JO ROYLE

You don't mess around when taking on the Pacific Ocean. Which is why Jo Royle, an experienced racer and instructor, was a great choice to pilot *Plastiki*. Jo, 30, has logged the kind of mileage on water—75,000-plus miles—normally associated with long-running vehicles. She has skippered for Formula 1 Sailing, raced the Transat Jacques Vabre from France to Brazil, and captained Earthwatch expeditions. But it was Jo's intense passion for the environment, demonstrated by her recently earning a master's degree in environmental science and society at the University of Central London, that made her the right co-skipper.

### WHO TAUGHT YOU ABOUT SAILING?

My dad gave me the passion, and then I learned a lot from sailing adventures with my first boyfriend. In my late teens, I delivered sailing boats long distances with a true salty named Trevor, which gave me really solid seamanship skills.

### IF NOT A SAILOR, WHAT WOULD YOU BE DOING?

Trapeze with Cirque du Soleil, although I doubt they'd have me.

### ANY SAILING OR ENVIRONMENTAL HEROES?

Many people have provided inspiration: yachtsman Peter Blake, marine biologist Sylvia Earle, and sailor and vagabond Bernard Moitessier.

### CHANGES YOU'VE SEEN IN THE MARINE ENVIRONMENT?

Signs of change are much more noticeable in the sub-Antarctic islands, where you see glacial retreat and bird colonies relocating farther south.

### OCEAN EXPLORATION OF OLD YOU WISH YOU'D BEEN ON?

Sailing the *Beagle* with Darwin in the time of the Fuegans, searching for new lands and new species. Imagine seeing the glaciated fjords without having seen pictures of them first.

### COOLEST THING ABOUT PLASTIKI?

I feel like a caretaker of the product of so many people's passion and creativity.

### IS YOUR ACTUAL HOME LARGER THAN PLASTIKI'S 14-BY-8-FOOT CABIN?

My home in Cornwall is smaller. I've spent a lot of time living on boats and other semi-outside dwellings. I like to make it a little hard to live. It makes you realize your connection to nature when you have to collect water, make electricity, etc.

### HOW'S YOUR DRIVING ON DRY LAND?

Who have you been talking to?

### ITEMS YOU TAKE ON EVERY TRIP?

Pen and paper, iPod, turquoise stone, an elephant, a seed, and an angle. The last four all fit in a tiny pouch.

us on an adventure that in my eyes was far greater than the physical crossing of the Pacific. We needed to find materials to build this superstructure. Andy proposed building the twin hulls and decking from marine-grade plywood—the crossbeams linking the hulls and supporting the cabin out of laminated, recycled timber—and the cabin out of corrugated iron.

A boat of marine-grade plywood and plastic bottles could make it across the Pacific, but would it set the world on fire? The final *Plastiki* looked a lot like Andy's boat, but our eventual materials would redefine *Plastiki*'s mission. More on that below.

It was a scaled-down prototype of Andy's design that was very nearly crushed by that coal barge in San Francisco Bay in June 2008, and me along with it. By that point, we had set up a small boat-building operation in Pier 31 along the San Francisco waterfront. The space was cavernous and chronically cold but perfect for what we needed—a boat-building lab. Matthew Grey, Adventure Ecology's expedition director, headed up the effort. A first-time visitor to Pier 31 would swear we were running some sort of bizarre recycling operation. Large bins of clear two-liter plastic bottles covered much of the floor space, as teams of volunteers carefully filled each bottle with a mysterious powdery substance before sealing it closed.

The powder poured into the bottles was dry ice—solid frozen carbon dioxide. It was Matthew's bright idea to strengthen the bottles this way. An empty soda bottle is plenty buoyant but rather flimsy. As the dry ice converted from a solid to gaseous state, the bottles would be internally pressurized and better able to withstand punishment from Pacific waves.

...

The most critical decision I could make affecting *Plastiki*'s chances of reaching Sydney was in the selection of a skipper. My hiring philosophy for *Plastiki* was to let people find us rather than seek them out. I believed *Plastiki* had incredible energy, its own kind of *Plastiki* karma. Jo Royle approached me through a mutual acquaintance at the Royal Geographical Society. Her sailing credentials were impeccable, with many years' experience at sea, but it was her passion for protecting the marine environment that stood out. Having just enrolled in a graduate program in environmental science, she wanted to make a difference. Jo and I instantly knew that *Plastiki* was the perfect match for her.

Jo soon enlisted David Thomson (known to all of us as "Mr. T") as co-skipper. Hiring an experienced co-skipper like David—a professional sailor for fourteen years and a member of four world record–setting racing teams—would allow Jo to sleep more soundly when she was off-watch, and I knew it would increase our chances of success. Assembling an expedition team is always tricky business, all the more so when six people will inhabit a seriously tiny cabin for many months. You want people on board who can not only get along, but who are dynamic, interesting, and bring a sense of magic. Not to mention have sailing skills. Finding candidates with all of the above skills? That would be dope.

My initial plan for the crew was to have a rotating cast of scientists, artists, athletes, and luminaries filling two of the six crew spots for two-week stints. Over time, the purity of a smaller team dedicated to the expedition held greater appeal. After the skippers, the crew we built consisted of Olav Heyerdahl, grandson of Thor; filmmakers Vern Moen and Max Jourdan; Graham Hill, founder of treehugger.com; Luca Babini, a talented photographer who had been following *Plastiki* for many months; and Singeli Agnew, who would take over filmmaking from Vern. I couldn't have asked for a nicer group.

In the adventure that was the making of *Plastiki*, December 10, 2009, stands out as one of the most historic and emotional days. That's when a giant crane arrived at Pier 31 to set our 12-ton plastic creation into San Francisco Bay. She floated! *Plastiki* was a full-fledged sailing vessel by this point, proudly displaying her distinctive geodesic-dome cabin and hulls filled with ranks of soda bottles. Much more work was yet to be done—electronics, rigging, and energy-generating systems—all of which would be accomplished at a boatyard across from San Francisco in Sausalito. Doubters and detractors of the project, of which there were many, carped about how long it had taken to build the boat and how far off schedule we were. The way I looked at it, the first two and a half years of the project were research and development, engineering the materials to build the boat. But admittedly my mistake was focusing more on the D than the R, which would create a host of challenges that ate up valuable time. The actual building process took only eight months, whereas it can take up to eighteen months or longer to build a typical boat.

*Plastiki* proved to be a seaworthy if lumbering vessel, as we found out during extensive trials in San Francisco Bay during January and February of 2010. We had no trouble attaining speeds of 6 knots, leading us to believe that with the help of trade winds, we could move at 8 knots. Without a daggerboard, the boat was considered

## PLASTIKI GEAR: NIKE BLAZER PYRATS

*Plastiki* employs up-to-the-minute technology, from the top of its mast (Inmarsat global satellite communications) down to the shoes on skipper Jo Royle's and David de Rothschild's feet. For Jo and David, Nike customized a water shoe version of its retro Blazer high-top to match their personalities and to handle life on a wet and slippery deck. Uppers of a polyester textile made with 50 percent recycled content, rubber treads that required no solvents or oil in their manufacture, and reduced cutting-room waste give the Pyrats a tiny environmental footprint.

Jo's sneaks have a light stone-colored upper, turquoise liner, and the three stars of Orion's belt adorning the heels. (Whenever she's at sea, Jo's parents look for the constellation to send her good vibes.) David's kicks are pirate black with a bloodred swoosh. Graphics of his dogs, Nesta and Smudge, decorate the heels.

BY NOVEMBER 2009, *PLASTIKI* WAS ESSENTIALLY
COMPLETE: SERETEX, 12,500 PLASTIC BOTTLES,
AND ONE BRIGHT ORANGE HORSESHOE
TO PRESERVE HER LUCK.

HERE COMES THE CRANE!!!
10:15 A.M. DECEMBER 10, 2009

10:58 A.M. DECEMBER 10, 2009

WE'RE

a "downwind" boat. At best, *Plastiki* could sail at 70 to 80 degrees into the wind. Tacking was out of the question. With a tailing wind, which we expected to encounter once we hit the equatorial trade winds, she excelled.

With each shakedown cruise, Jo and David, under the watchful eyes of Andy Dovell and boat builder Andy Fox, pushed *Plastiki* a bit harder. The true test came on February 18: We sailed through the Golden Gate and out into the Pacific for the first time. Through big swells and wind blasting to 30 knots, *Plastiki* shone. The same could not be said for me. It would appear I inherited my father's inner-ear deficiency on open water, since I spent the three days at sea wretchedly sick. At three o'clock one morning, while puking over the side of the boat in a freezing wind and tossing sea, the thought did occur to me, "What the hell am I doing?" Seasickness couldn't last forever (could it?), so it was something I'd just have to deal with when the real voyage started.

Would Seretex, the special material we had created to build our boat, withstand months of assault from wind, waves, salt, and sun to remain intact and deliver us to Sydney? Would the boat's plastic welds and nut-and-sugar-based epoxy hold fast? And what of the crew? Would the fast friendships and camaraderie survive more than one hundred days at sea? *Plastiki* sailed beneath the Golden Gate Bridge one final time on March 20, 2010, auspiciously on the spring equinox. Between bouts of nausea, I felt a sense of pride. We were being escorted by dozens of boats with loved ones waving and cheering. My head full of unanswered questions, I recognized the pangs of anxiety that signaled the true adventure had now begun. At least one thing was certain: The boat made of plastic bottles sailed true.

CAPTAIN JO ROYLE STEERS THE NEWLY LAUNCHED
*PLASTIKI* TOWARD ITS BERTH IN SAUSALITO.

# FROM POMEGRANATES TO PLASTIKI: HOW BIOMIMICRY HELPED BUILD THE BOAT

### BY MICHAEL PAWLYN

I met David de Rothschild at the Google Zeitgeist conference in 2007, where we both spoke during the session about green technology. He explained his idea of the *Plastiki* expedition, and I was immediately captivated. It had exactly the right combination of elements to appeal to my interests: eccentricity, high idealism, and a clear determination to bring about positive change.

I had not previously heard about the Pacific garbage patches, and I was struck by the way that they represented a very powerful metaphor for the way we treat the oceans—we behave as if the sea has a limitless capacity to absorb our pollution, and as long as it is out of sight we're not bothered.

David and I shared an interest in the "cradle-to-cradle" concept developed by William McDonough and Michael Braungart that proposes a way in which we can shift from a linear way of using resources to one that keeps all resources in closed cycles so nothing is wasted and no pollution is emitted. Ecosystems present a great model of closed-loop systems in which any waste from one organism becomes the nutrient for something else. We can learn a lot from the way that natural systems work in rethinking our own systems and designing out the whole concept of waste.

The brief for *Plastiki* was to design a boat made out of plastic bottles that could sail across the Pacific Ocean and that would draw attention to the problems facing the oceans as well as to the kind of solutions that we need to implement.

We agreed that, to set the right example,

the boat should be designed to be fully recyclable at the end of the journey, generate all its own energy, and emit no pollution. We also felt that the bottles should be used intact rather than simply melted down into a sheet material and turned into a conventional boat.

The first challenge was to find a way to turn a very weak material (plastic bottles) into a structure that would withstand the forces likely to be experienced on a voyage through the Pacific Ocean.

We took our inspiration from a number of examples that included the way that eggs used to be packaged in Japan (tied together with reeds so that the eggs are held firmly in compression) and the traditional structures built entirely out of bundles of grass. Both were examples of how, with design ingenuity, something flimsy or fragile can be turned into something robust.

However, the source that provided the greatest breakthrough was a pomegranate. When I was cutting one up, I realized that each individual segment had a degree of internal pressure, and that by packing them together in a geometrically compact way, filling the gaps with pith, and surrounding them all with a tough skin, the end result is a very resilient form.

This led to the idea of pressurizing each bottle with air—a simple move that transformed the bottles into incredibly solid objects. In our tests we proved that just by adding air pressure it was possible for two plastic bottles to support

the weight of a car.

It was very satisfying to see the concepts of biomimicry being taken through the whole project, including the design of the cabin by Nathaniel Corum of Architecture for Humanity and the first use of a completely nontoxic type of glue as an alternative to the conventional resin-based compounds used in boat building.

David's determination for the project to be about solutions rather than just highlighting problems has resulted in a range of inspiring closed-loop design examples. This shows that, with the right attitude, it is possible to design out waste and to rethink the way we use resources to create far more intelligent solutions.

There are two profound shifts we need to make: from linear to closed-loop design and from a carbon economy to a solar economy. Biomimicry has provided, and will continue to provide, many of the solutions that we need, and with projects like *Plastiki* we can bring about positive change. I'm proud to have played a part in making it a reality.

· · ·

*Michael Pawlyn is the director of Exploration Architecture, an innovative design and solutions company that helped design* Plastiki.

# 2

## DESIGNING PLASTIKI

BUILDING *PLASTIKI* WAS PART OF THE ADVENTURE, EXPLORING THE UNCHARTED AND SPARSELY POPULATED EDGES OF PLASTIC TECHNOLOGY.

BUILDING A SAILBOAT IS ALL ABOUT MAXIMIZING SPEED AND AGILITY.
FOR BOAT DESIGNERS, THAT TRANSLATES INTO A NEVER-ENDING QUEST
FOR LIGHTER, STRONGER MATERIALS AND LESS DRAG IN THE WATER.
THE RESULT IS USUALLY A SLEEK AND FAST PLEASURE CRAFT.

*Plastiki* didn't play by the same set of rules. Practically everything about her was unconventional, if not verging on heretical. All recycled or borrowed or newly invented parts, *Plastiki* might not have been streamlined or fleet, but she was brimming with cutting-edge technology nonetheless. And to my eye, she was beautiful.

Any sailor looking at our ship could see that crossing the Pacific swiftly was not our prime objective. If it had been, we could have built our boat out of fiberglass and called it a day. Instead, we viewed *Plastiki* as a metaphor for solutions to the problem of plastic flotsam—really, the problem of plastic *everywhere*. *Plastiki* became a floating test platform for solutions. More than any other element of the expedition, *Plastiki* herself represented our goals—she became a metaphor for change.

The farther we got into designing and building, the more we discovered that the easy way was invariably the conventional way. And the conventional way was always the dirtiest, most wasteful way. Real innovation came by avoiding the path of least resistance.

It's that mind-set that led our team to Michael Pawlyn and a design approach that mimicked the natural world. It's what led us to collect and pressurize 12,500 secondhand soda bottles. It's what made Matt Grey and me develop serious misgivings about building the boat's skeleton and decking from plain old timber and plywood. In a nod to *Kon-Tiki*, we even considered building with bamboo or balsa. None of those options felt right—it could be any boat in the world. Wasn't the whole point of *Plastiki* to showcase smart thinking, uninhibited curiosity, and new ideas? We had to do better.

Boat designers like *Plastiki*'s Andy Dovell prize strong materials that can withstand the powerful forces exerted by waves and wind. Fiberglass, aluminum, and carbon fiber are their building blocks of choice. But each of those is the product of a wasteful, polluting system. They require huge amounts of energy to make, and with the exception of aluminum, they're destined for landfills at the end of their life. We were convinced there was a material out there that would sync with *Plastiki*'s goals and still get the job done. To be consistent with the

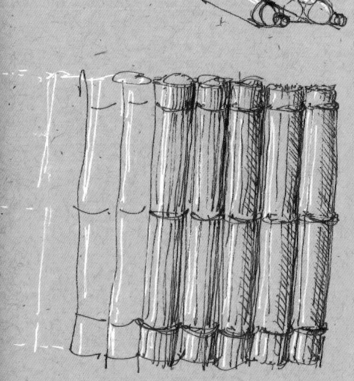

MICHAEL PAWLYN DESIGNED BUNDLES OF
BUOYANT BOTTLES INSPIRED BY THE INTERIOR
STRUCTURE OF A POMEGRANATE.

HOW TO MAKE srPET AT HOME

1. Tape up a foam sandwich, attach wires

2. Cook sandwich at proper temperature

3. Collect off-gassing with a hose. Hope landlord doesn't smell it.

cradle-to-cradle model of "upcycling" espoused by architect and green guru William McDonough, we wanted to use a plastic designed with its full life span in mind, so it could be entirely recycled. We wanted a material that embodied the idea that waste is a design flaw, not the natural order of things. As Matt put it, "All that was now left to do was find that perfect material."

Andy already had his hands full before we upped the ante by committing to a plastic superstructure. We continued to feed him outlandish ideas that he variously absorbed, integrated, and deflected with good grace. Now we were asking him to build with trash. Andy had

> THE FIRST AND MAYBE LAST THING YOU NEED TO KNOW IS THAT THE [PLASTICS] BUSINESS IS GEARED TOWARD MAKING PRODUCTS THAT LAST FOREVER BUT ARE USED FOR ONLY A SHORT TIME. IT'S LUNACY.

never worked with recycled plastic before—what boat designer had?—but he was game to try. "Working in recycled plastics presented a massive hurdle because these materials are typically low strength due to the different types of chemistries thrown together," he said. "It's usually a dog's lunch of polypropylene, HDPE, vinyl, and polyethylene."

Our first foray into the still-evolving world of engineered plastics turned up EcoBoard, a recycled plastic lumber made of 100 percent polyethylene. If you're building a deck or playground equipment, I highly recommend it. If you're building an oceangoing boat to withstand 50 mph winds and seas to match, then its lack of rigidity is a nonstarter. We later uncovered a plastic alternative to plywood, EcoSheet, advertised as being

"as strong as plywood and made entirely from mixed recycled plastics." With few—or no!—other options on the table, we ordered a load. The moment we pulled it off the truck, we knew it was wrong. It was heavy and bendable. Andy wanted nothing to do with it. "Might as well build with lead," he said.

Searching for the right material, I learned a lot about the plastic industry. The first and maybe last thing you need to know is that the entire business is geared toward making products that last forever but are used for only a short time. It's lunacy.

It was clear that no one had gotten serious about making high-performance, upcycleable plastics. We were going to have to innovate our way to *Plastiki*. Matt and our first boat builder, Mike Rose, flew to Europe, the hotbed of recycled-plastics R&D, and set off on a 2,000-mile tour of potential manufacturers in Germany, Denmark, and the Netherlands. They met with several companies that make a strong, lightweight plastic cloth called "structurally reinforced polypropylene," which would have suited us in a pinch. But the more we thought about it, the more particular we became about the type of plastic our boat would be built from. Polypropylene is used in food containers. We wanted an engineered plastic composed of polyethylene terephthalate (PET), the plastic in water and soda bottles. Only it didn't seem to exist.

WAITING FOR THE RESULT TO COME BACK FOR OUR srPET—CAN WE CONTINUE TO BUILD?
@DREXPLORE 11:05 A.M., MARCH 29, 2009

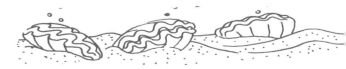

*PLASTIKI* REQUIRED LOADS OF NOT-QUITE-RAW MATERIALS: USED SOFT-DRINK BOTTLES, BROUGHT BY THE CARLOAD.

Matt and Mike finally got lucky in Denmark. A small firm, Comfil, makes a woven fabric called "structurally reinforced PET" (srPET). It's light, superstrong, and fully recyclable. That's important—a lot of materials *appear* recyclable but have some additive or chemical that turns them into unusable rubbish. If we could get pure PET out of *Plastiki* after the expedition, it could be upcycled into a thousand different products. "We had no real data on the srPET," recalls Matt. "The manufacturers themselves knew very little about it, and certainly nobody had ever dreamed of making a 60-foot boat out of it. We were very much on our own with the stuff, which seemed to be in perfect keeping with the pioneering spirit of the adventure." What could be more fitting an illustration of "waste as resource" than a boat floating on plastic bottles with a structure made from a unique engineering plastic also made from plastic bottles?

Matt and Mike left Denmark with the only two rolls of srPET in the world tucked under their arms. It turns out that srPET has been around since the mid-1980s, but there had never been a reason to take it out of the workshop. Why would the plastics industry, which is devoted to one-time use, want to develop a single substance plastic with the potential for upcycling?

As a fabric, srPET on its own wouldn't be of much use to us. But as the stiff "bread" in a foam-core sandwich, it could deliver a panel with a remarkable strength-to-weight ratio. The foam "meat" would come from a new PET foam made by Alcan Composites (now called 3A Composites USA). Now all we had to do was figure out a way to get the srPET to stick to the foam without the benefit of epoxy, the kind of additive that would ruin its recyclability.

• • •

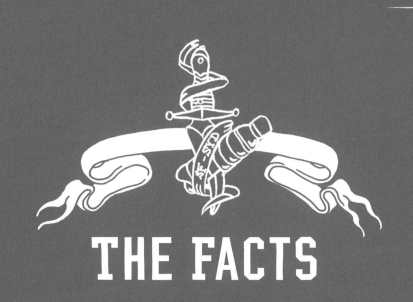

# THE FACTS

17 MILLION BARRELS OF CRUDE OIL ARE USED
TO MAKE THE 29 BILLION PLASTIC BOTTLES
AMERICANS CONSUME EACH YEAR.

FIVE OF EVERY SIX PLASTIC WATER BOTTLES
ARE NOT RECYCLED.

A PLASTIC BOTTLE CAN TAKE 450 YEARS
TO DEGRADE.

## STUCK ON BIO-GLUE

Sail across the Pacific in a boat glued together with by-products of stuff you'd find in the kitchen cupboard? Are you nuts? As a matter of fact, yes. Critical joinery on *Plastiki* is reinforced or held together entirely by an epoxy made from cashew nut oil and molasses sludge.

A polymer is a polymer, whether derived from a plant source or more commonly from petroleum, says Mike O'Reilly, who helped invent the compound. "You can get polymers from milk, flax oil, or soybean oil. It's just less prevalent. For an engineer to pick a bio-polymer, he'd really want to have to go that route," says O'Reilly.

The *Plastiki* team wanted to go that route. In the cashew-sugar epoxy formulation, long-chain polymers derived from molasses sludge, a waste product from sugar refining, make up the resin component. Nutshell oil, chemically similar to ammonia, is the hardener. In all, 25 gallons of the cashew-sugar epoxy were used on *Plastiki*. "This is the future of the adhesives industry," says O'Reilly.

If the cooking odors emanating from 760 Chestnut Street in San Francisco's North Beach section in the summer of 2008 were unusual, that's because the crew from Adventure Ecology was inside playing chef with plastic. We would crank up the oven to different temperatures, toss in a sandwich of srPET fabric and PET foam, and see what developed. Cathodes stuck into the foam let us know whether or not we achieved uniform heating. The results weren't always pretty, but we learned some important things: For one, with some refinement, we'd be able to meld the two plastic materials together just fine, and two, the aroma of melting PET seems to linger forever. *Ding*—there goes the rental deposit on the apartment!

---

## PLASTIKI'S MORE IMPORTANT EXPLORATION HAS BEEN AT THE OUTER EDGE OF SUSTAINABLE MATERIALS.

---

No one had worked with srPET the way we were, and our learning curve with the material was steep and painful and smelly. Woven srPET fabric consists of two types of fibers with different melting points. The idea is to apply enough heat to melt the matrix fibers but not enough to melt the high-tenacity fibers. The matrix then consolidates around the high-tenacity fiber, which remains unmelted and able to support the structure.

Through constant experimentation with our novel plastics, we hit on a winning recipe. It went like this: Put four layers of srPET cloth on top of a PET foam panel, put four layers on the bottom, insert that sandwich into a vacuum bag, put the bag in a press at 52 pounds of pressure per square inch, and heat to 390 degrees

BOTTLES WERE CLEANED, FILLED WITH
CARBON DIOXIDE, AND THEN HEAT SEALED
WITH THE CASHEW-BASED NUT-GU.

Fahrenheit. In time, the results we achieved with this new material were so consistent and high performing that we dubbed it Seretex and applied for trademark protection. When tested at an engineering lab in New Zealand, Seretex could withstand the forces generated by 70-knot winds and huge seas.

It had taken the better part of a year to produce the equivalent of a piece of plywood you might pick up at Home Depot. By Matt's estimate, we were just 5 percent of the way toward completing the boat. Still, in December 2008, we announced our intention to launch on April 28, 2009, the same day *Kon-Tiki* set sail in 1947. It was an audacious stunt given how far along we actually were. Articles about *Plastiki* soon appeared in *Outside* magazine, the *New Yorker*, *USA Today*, and other outlets. It was the beginning of a two-year wave of press that called attention to our expedition and its

goals. And it was the beginning of two years of "Why haven't you left yet?" questions.

If I have a regret, it is that I didn't make it plainer to the media that we weren't so much building a boat as engineering the materials necessary to build it. This is still a challenge: Yes, *Plastiki* is about an expedition across the Pacific. But its more important exploration has been at the outer edge of sustainable materials.

Once we had the materials dialed in, the actual building of *Plastiki* was accomplished in record time. Using the equipment on hand at Pier 31, we could fabricate the flat panels that would eventually become *Plastiki*'s geodesic cabin. The boat's bigger structural components—the 20-foot-long cross-beams and 60-foot-long backbone for each hull—were beyond our capabilities. We needed a really big press and precision molds, among other specialty machinery.

# CREW PROFILE: DAVID THOMSON

The only office Mr. T knows is the rolling deck of a sailboat in mid-ocean. He's a professional racer who likes to go fast and go long. The open ocean is where he feels most at home. In 2009, he circled the globe in a 40-foot sailboat, just him and another sailor, in the Portimao Global Ocean Race. He was a crew member on *Playstation*, a giant catamaran that set four world records. David wasn't an environmentalist before joining *Plastiki*, but that's changed. "My eyes are open to the problems the oceans have," he says.

### HOW MANY MONTHS WILL YOU SPEND AT SEA IN A YEAR?
I've been at sea for about six months a year the last few years.

### WHAT HAVE YOU GOT AGAINST DRY LAND?
Nothing, but what I love about being at sea is there are few rules: You do what you want. I think life on land has become a police society, which I hate.

### WHAT WAS YOUR FIRST SAILING BOAT?
A small catamaran my father bought us kids when I was about twelve years old.

### WHO TAUGHT YOU THE MOST ABOUT SAILING?
My brother, Alex Thomson, and Josh Hall, *Plastiki*'s safety manager, who has been a huge influence in my sailing career and helped steer me in the right direction.

### IF NOT A SAILOR, WHAT WOULD YOU BE?
I always wanted to be a professional rugby player. And I almost joined the Royal Marines.

### COOLEST THING ABOUT THE PLASTIKI MISSION?
Being able to get the message across to so many people.

### BIGGEST PERSONAL CHALLENGE ON PLASTIKI?
Dealing with the mental issues in my head because we were going so slow!

### BIGGEST NAUTICAL CHALLENGE ON PLASTIKI?
Keeping the sails together and the mast upright.

### WILL YOU EVER LOOK AT A PLASTIC BOTTLE THE SAME WAY AGAIN?
No way. I hope to get plastic bags and Styrofoam banned from my hometown when I get back.

### FASTEST YOU'VE GONE UNDER SAIL POWER?
About 36.6 knots on Steve Fosset's *Playstation*, a 120-foot catamaran.

### WORST STORM YOU'VE EVER BEEN IN?
I got myself into an 80-knot storm in the Southern Ocean last year. Not a place I want to get myself into again. Imagine a Mavericks-type wave but over and over and over again, and the feeling of not making it through the other side.

### ITEM YOU TAKE ON EVERY SAILING TRIP?
Marmite (it tastes so good), pics of the family, and chocolate.

EXPEDITION DIRECTOR MATTHEW GREY TESTED AN EARLY STRUCTURAL DESIGN USING BAMBOO AND TWINE (TOP LEFT) AND HELPED BUILD THE PLYWOOD-AND-PLASTIC-BOTTLE PROTOTYPE.

Matt pulled out the phone book and started dialing. Here's an instance of the good karma that surrounded *Plastiki:* One of the first companies Matt dialed was Level 2 Industries, a San Francisco firm specializing in industrial design and material science and which has founded such companies as Glissade Snowboards and Bender Brothers. On the other end of the line was Greg Pronko, managing partner, who was in Kauai with business partner Mike O'Reilly at the company's surf retreat, called Tiki House. In what can be considered a divine

HERE WE WERE LATE TO LAUNCH, NECK-DEEP IN DEVELOPING A NEW PLASTIC MATERIAL, AND WE HAD NO BOAT BUILDER? WERE WE OUT OF OUR MINDS?

coincidence, Mike was at that moment reading Thor Heyerdahl's book *Kon-Tiki.* After the call, Greg turned to Mike and said, "I think your book just called me."

From that auspicious start, our partnership with Level 2 (though we called them Bender Brothers) kicked production on *Plastiki* into high gear. With the loan of a 5-ton compression press for making snowboards, Matt guided a team in making those long hull panels. They slid each panel into a 60-foot-long vacuum bag, then fed the panel through the heated press at a rate of four inches every five minutes. It took eighteen hours for each hull panel to complete the journey. It was exhausting and nerve-wracking work, since a tiny leak in the vacuum bag could ruin $10,000 worth of srPET and PET foam.

•••

As the work inside Pier 31 began to yield tangible results, relations among team members frayed. A contest of wills developed between Matt and Mike Rose.

The situation became toxic and confusing for project members who were given contradictory orders from Matt and Mike. With the announced launch date already come and gone, I had to make the decision to let Mike go in February 2009.

Here we were late to launch, neck-deep in developing a new plastic material, and we had no boat builder? Were we out of our minds?

As it turned out, the energy level on the team soared, and production did, too. We felt newly free to tinker, make mistakes, and ask questions. It was late nights and beers and total commitment. By April, we had a new boat builder, Andy Fox, a Brit with extensive experience constructing racing catamarans and working with thermoplastics. He had even worked on Michael Pawlyn's Eden Project, a nice bit of synchronicity. "We don't need you to tinker," I told him at the outset. "We need you to start building." He went ahead and tinkered anyway, which turns out to have been exactly what we needed. He and Matt figured out a way to use heat guns to bond individual panels together and to build I-beams out of Seretex for the boat's skeleton. With those structural components, the boat took shape.

Without a doubt, one of *Plastiki's* most visually arresting features was its cabin. It looked futuristic and retro at the same time, and it instantly announced to everyone who saw it that ours was a boat like no other. To design the cabin, I turned to Nathaniel Corum, architect and head of education outreach at Architecture for Humanity. On a typical oceangoing catamaran, living quarters are located below deck in the large hulls. We couldn't get away with that since our hulls were not hollow, and neither would we have wanted to. Our cabin had to be prominent and iconic.

Among several options Nathaniel brought back to us was the clever egg-shaped structure that would eventually grace *Plastiki.* I was instantly drawn to its geodesic shape, as I'm a big fan of Buckminster Fuller. "In

A PROTOTYPE OF WHAT WOULD BECOME
*PLASTIKI* WAS LAUNCHED IN JUNE 2009.
EXCEPT FOR A NEAR MISS WITH A TUGBOAT,
IT WAS A GREAT SUCCESS.

terms of inspiration, it falls between a 'Bucky Ball' and biomimicry," said Nathaniel, "because I used horseshoe crab shells and the fused plates of turtle shells for geometric reference." His 12-foot-wide, 23-foot-long dome would be self-supporting and incredibly strong and would make maximal use of the tight clearance beneath the boom of the mainsail and the decking area between the hulls. Within its 200 square feet of floor space, a crew of six or seven would cook, eat, sleep, blog, and communicate with the outside world. And you thought an efficiency apartment in New York City was cramped.

Executing Nathaniel's vision taxed the significant

MY CREDO THROUGHOUT THE BUILD WAS "NOBODY KNOWS AS MUCH AS EVERYBODY." IN MY WILDEST DREAMS I COULDN'T HAVE IMAGINED WHERE THIS AMAZING JOURNEY INTO CURIOSITY WOULD LEAD.

skills and brainpower of Matt, Andy, and the Bender Brothers. In all, 134 triangles of Seretex made up the cabin, each with fifteen different angles that had to align with its neighbors. Rather than cut individual panels, Greg Pronko and the rest of the team decided to make origami-style folds in long pieces of Seretex, each fold made possible by a precisely calculated V-cut on one side of the fabric. They reasoned that assembly would be easier and the risk of leaky seams minimized. With 2,010 separate angles to calculate and fold, and very little Seretex material remaining, our build team had no room for error. They had to get it right on the first try.

. . .

Experimentation and new thinking were woven into every facet of *Plastiki*. Where the force loads were going to be greatest on the boat's skeleton—at the base of the masts and where the 20-foot crossbeams attached to the hulls—we reinforced key joints with an innovative bio-epoxy the Bender Brothers had home brewed. Their concoction was derived not from a typical petroleum base but from cashew nut oil and molasses sludge. To the uninitiated—namely me—holding a boat together with nuts and sugar sounded preposterous, but Mike Bender convinced us that a plant-based polymer would be just as effective as a petroleum-based polymer (see "Stuck on Bio-Glue," page 46). Besides, as Mike pointed out, "using a petroleum epoxy was a cheating way to get through the project."

The headsail, in effect our boat's engine, was made of postconsumer PET spun into a heavy-duty fabric. So new was the idea of recycled sailcloth that our sail was the world's first made from it. When Pineapple Sails in Alameda, California, was finished cutting and sewing, the half yard of sailcloth on the shop floor represented the last known quantity of that cloth.

Both masts were reincarnated from piping used in irrigation booms—not your typical mast-making material. The odd-looking chamber welded to the mizzenmast (rear mast) was a rotating cylinder garden that housed ninety-eight vegetable plants. The garden would supply the crew with fresh chard, kale, spinach, bok choy, mustard, and other leafy greens (no scurvy for us!).

Where some of the sharpest thinking was brought

INVESTIGATING A WAY TO TURN OUR PLASTIKI POOP INTO FUEL CELL TECHNOLOGY!!
@DREXPLORE 9:04 A.M., JULY 24, 2009

AFTER SUCCESSFULLY MAKING SMALL BATCHES
OF SERETEX, THE NEXT STEP WAS TO MAKE HUGE
PIECES OF IT, WHICH WOULD BECOME
THE BOAT'S STRUCTURE.

BOAT BUILDER ANDY FOX (LEFT), HERE WITH DAVID DE ROTHSCHILD, JOINED THE TEAM IN APRIL 2009 AND QUICKLY HELPED COMPLETE *PLASTIKI*'S STRUCTURAL PLAN.

to bear was on *Plastiki*'s renewable energy system. Our electricity needs were sizable, as we would be firing up an Inmarsat satellite navigation system and several HP Probook 5310s, as well as recharging cameras, flashlights, and everyone's iPods, iPhones, BlackBerries, my and David T's GameBoys, and other gadgets. We needed a robust power system that was self-sustaining without resorting to a diesel-powered generator, as most sailboats do.

Working with designer Jason Iftakhar, we devised triangular solar panels that conformed to the pie-shape wedges on the roof of the boat's cabin. Solar panels are usually square, so reconfiguring them was no easy feat. The rooftop photovoltaics would deliver 420 watts of juice. Four pivoting solar panels mounted at the stern would kick in another 800 watts. Rounding out our power supply were twin wind turbines that could contribute roughly 40 watts when really cranking, and an energy bike mounted near the bow that created just enough electricity to run the boat's stereo system. (Another benefit of the bike: It prevented the crew from developing a sailor's chicken legs.) A plan to drag a power-generating sea turbine behind the boat was dropped after sea trials in San Francisco Bay when it became evident that *Plastiki* would rarely top the 6-knot-per-hour speed required by that device. A bank of six 12-volt batteries stored the electric charge.

As any committed off-the-grid homesteader in northern California might tell you, when the only electricity available is self-generated, you become acutely aware of use and of living within your limits. A hierarchy of need develops quickly. Aboard *Plastiki*, each of us was personally invested in tracking the boat's stored energy supply. There was always enough juice for vital functions

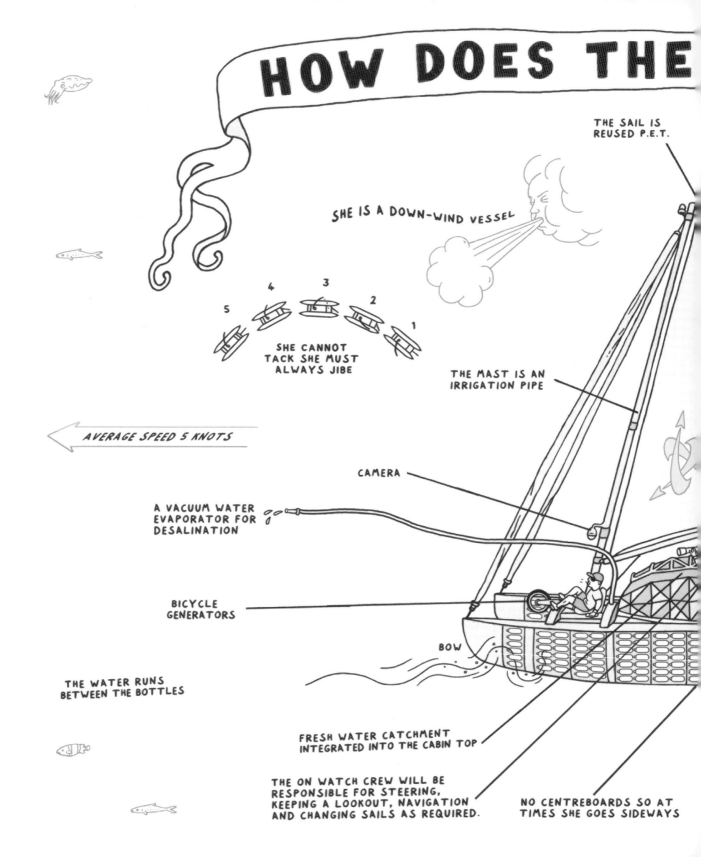

# HOW DOES THE

THE SAIL IS
REUSED P.E.T.

SHE IS A DOWN-WIND VESSEL

4   3
5        2
            1

SHE CANNOT
TACK SHE MUST
ALWAYS JIBE

THE MAST IS AN
IRRIGATION PIPE

AVERAGE SPEED 5 KNOTS

CAMERA

A VACUUM WATER
EVAPORATOR FOR
DESALINATION

BICYCLE
GENERATORS

BOW

THE WATER RUNS
BETWEEN THE BOTTLES

FRESH WATER CATCHMENT
INTEGRATED INTO THE CABIN TOP

THE ON WATCH CREW WILL BE
RESPONSIBLE FOR STEERING,
KEEPING A LOOKOUT, NAVIGATION
AND CHANGING SAILS AS REQUIRED.

NO CENTREBOARDS SO AT
TIMES SHE GOES SIDEWAYS

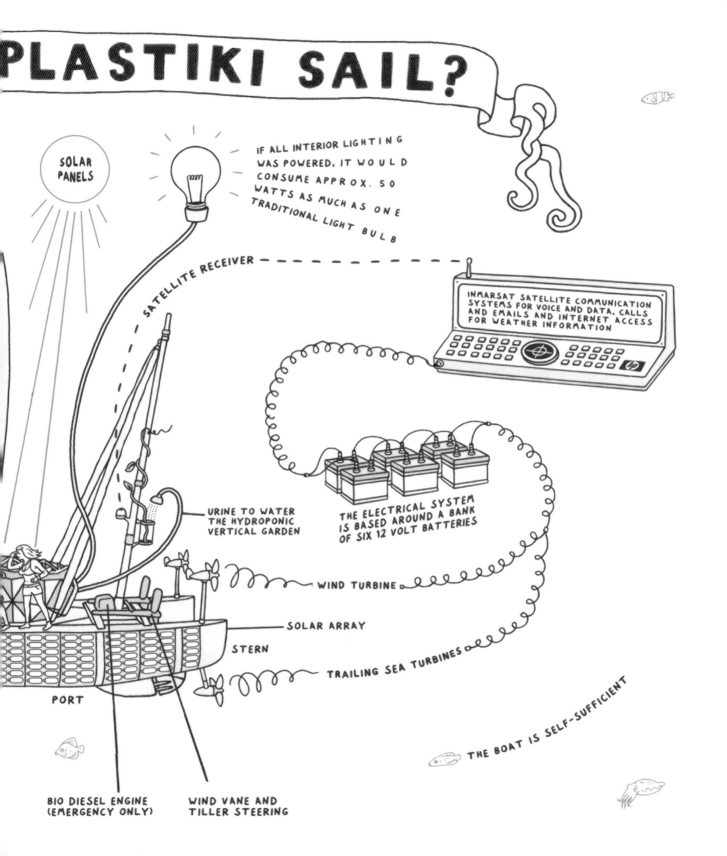

# PLASTIKI SAIL?

SOLAR PANELS

IF ALL INTERIOR LIGHTING WAS POWERED, IT WOULD CONSUME APPROX. 50 WATTS AS MUCH AS ONE TRADITIONAL LIGHT BULB

SATELLITE RECEIVER

INMARSAT SATELLITE COMMUNICATION SYSTEMS FOR VOICE AND DATA, CALLS AND EMAILS AND INTERNET ACCESS FOR WEATHER INFORMATION

URINE TO WATER THE HYDROPONIC VERTICAL GARDEN

THE ELECTRICAL SYSTEM IS BASED AROUND A BANK OF SIX 12 VOLT BATTERIES

WIND TURBINE

SOLAR ARRAY

STERN

TRAILING SEA TURBINES

PORT

THE BOAT IS SELF-SUFFICIENT

BIO DIESEL ENGINE (EMERGENCY ONLY)

WIND VANE AND TILLER STEERING

like daily satellite communication with our safety crew in Australia and running navigation software on the laptops. However, when cloud cover or low sun angle limited recharging of the solar panels, as was the case in the first few weeks of our journey, it meant forgoing music, e-mail, and digital entertainment. And believe me, that led to some long night watches. As soon as we reached the strong sun and steady winds of the tropics, we no longer had to worry about our electricity stores.

• • •

Building *Plastiki* required such unorthodox innovation that it could be accomplished only through collective thought and collective skills. I realized from the very start that I was never going to be able to do it on my own, so I embraced an open-source approach. The more ideas—and the crazier—the better. My credo throughout the build was "Nobody knows as much as everybody." In my wildest dreams I couldn't have imagined where this amazing journey into curiosity would lead.

*PLASTIKI* LEFT SAUSALITO FOR SEA TRIALS AT DAWN, LOADED WITH PLENTY OF SAILORS AND FRIENDS.

## SAILING TOWARD A STRATEGY OF HOPE IN
## THE LAND OF MANY-COLORED THINGS

### BY WILLIAM MCDONOUGH

In our book, *Cradle to Cradle,* chemist Michael Braungart and I asked readers to imagine an assignment: You have been given the challenge of designing the Industrial Revolution—retrospectively. With respect to its negative consequences, the assignment would have to read something like this:

Design a system of production that puts billions of pounds of toxic material into the air, water, and soil every year; produces some materials so dangerous they will require constant vigilance by future generations; results in gigantic amounts of waste; puts valuable materials in holes all over the planet, where they can never be retrieved; requires thousands of complex regulations—not to keep people and natural systems safe, but to keep them from being poisoned too

quickly; measures productivity by how few people are working; creates prosperity by digging up or cutting down natural resources and then burying or burning them; and erodes the diversity of species and cultural practices.

As a result of research in the past decade and the brave explorations of Captain Charles Moore, we might have to add to the above list: puts plastics in the ocean, specifically the North Pacific gyres, where the ratio of plastic to zooplankton is 36:1.

Thirty-six times as much plastic as plankton! What are we doing to the planet?

What David de Rothschild and the *Plastiki* expedition have called to our attention is a massive design problem. What better way to address that problem than with something that is new and ancient at the same time—an epic voyage. And with a vessel that is homeopathic. A small dose of the very thing we wish to avoid: plastic in the ocean.

In ancient Ireland, where my ancestors come from, there were worlds beyond this world. There was Faery, a land of the little people, the giants, and the banshees. It appeared exactly the same as this world, just a little bit better—an important concept for a melancholy race.

The world to which we would move after we left this life, Tír na nÓg, got a bit better. The people who inhabit it are "the forever young" because they do not age. They call us "the immortals" because we have children and they cannot. They expect and are waiting for Armageddon. For them, the world will end in an instant. They live as if there is no tomorrow, because there might not be.

Our culture has been living as if we are forever young. We throw things "away" as if there is no tomorrow. The plastics in the gyres are the detritus of our unthinking exuberance on one hand, but perhaps our terror on the other. Why would we live like this?

Perhaps it has something to do with Einstein's special theory of relativity. $E=mc^2$ was one of the great discoveries of the past century, but we have not fully integrated its implications. Humans could be facing Armageddon with little warning, just as those in Hiroshima and Nagasaki did in 1945. In the course of human experience, this is a new possibility. Over the past sixty years, perhaps we have started living as if there is no tomorrow. Perhaps we have acted as if we didn't have children, as if future generations were not a consideration.

Beyond Tír na nÓg is the Land of Many-Colored Things. No one has returned from the Land of Many-Colored Things. The presumption is that it's too beautiful to leave. The way to the Land of Many-Colored Things was over the western horizon. The ancients would get in a *curragh*, a keeless seal-skin boat, and sail to the west.

David de Rothschild set forth in a strange and wonderful vessel from the West Coast of North America. His goal was hopeful: to move toward a world where everything was a little bit better. He was in the ocean where the forever young, who lived as if there is no tomorrow, cast their detritus—intentionally or unintentionally. He moved through vast expanses, directed by an internal compass (and probably some support from a GPS) and sailed on to his Land of Many Colored Things. He returns to us from over the horizon to tell us his stories. And the world gets better.

...

*William McDonough is an internationally renowned architect. He and the German chemist Dr. Michael Braungart co-authored* Cradle to Cradle: Remaking the Way We Make Things, *which has been translated into ten languages.*

# 3

SUNRISE OVER A SYNTHETIC SEA

AFTER YEARS OF WORK, *PLASTIKI*
SAILED UNDER THE GOLDEN GATE FOR THE
LAST TIME. SHE WOULD SOON BE TESTED BY
THE POWER OF THE PACIFIC.

A DECIDED ADVANTAGE OF A DOWNWIND VESSEL IS THAT IT
LEAVES NO CHANCE OF TURNING BACK. HITCH INTO THE FLOW OF WIND
AND CURRENTS, AND AWAY YOU GO. THAT PARTICULAR ASPECT
OF PLASTIKI WOULD PROVE ESPECIALLY USEFUL IN THE
PREDAWN HOURS OF OUR FOURTH DAY AT SEA.

I was on deck with David Thomson and Vern at the time, and not by choice. We had drawn the 1:00 to 4:00 A.M. shift, an arrangement dictated by the schedule of watches set up by our skipper, Jo. It's a fact of nautical life that somebody must be at the helm at all times, night and day. With two experienced sailors aboard and four "land crabs," it made sense to organize two watch teams captained by David, aka "Mr. T," and Jo. Three hours on, three hours off—a routine that quickly yields the kind of physical and mental exhaustion known to parents of a colicky newborn.

The three of us were chattering away, bundled in our wool caps and every scrap of clothing we owned to ward off the chill, when the wind, previously a light easterly breeze flowing out from Baja California, in Mexico, shifted suddenly to a tempest barreling down from the Gulf of Alaska. A cold front had whipped through. The sea, so placid for three days, changed character in an instant. Massive swells reared up and then crashed down over us. We were tossed around the back of the boat like bath toys. I was at the tiller when out of the dark

came a towering wave that knocked me from one side of the boat to the other. Only my grip on the tiller and being clipped to the safety line running the length of the boat prevented me from being swept overboard into the maelstrom.

The chaos of surf and spray was exhilarating at first. "Yes," I thought, "this is what crossing the Pacific is supposed to be all about. Wind. Waves. Spray." But after an hour of me being tossed and doused, the novelty wore thin. Tentacles of icy seawater snuck past my waterproof outer layers. Fatigue, brought on by bracing every muscle against the impact of onrushing water, was setting in. And I could feel my old nemesis, the queasiness of seasickness, beginning to build. "Okay, enough with the waves! We can stop now." No such luck. The pounding wouldn't relent for forty-eight hours.

There's an old saying about seasickness that, after much personal experience, I can say rings true: You start off worrying that you might die. After a while, you worry that you won't. I knew this bout was coming, dreaded it even. I feared a repetition of the sea trials, of being

ON THE MORNING OF MARCH 20, 2010, WITH A
FINAL WAVE FROM DAVID DE ROTHSCHILD, *PLASTIKI*
SAID GOODBYE TO HER ESCORTS AND WAS
ON HER WAY TO AUSTRALIA.

horrifically sick, unable to move, and really wanting to put an end to my misery by jumping into the water. Or turning the boat around. But this go-around I came prepared. I right away stuck a Dramamine patch behind one ear and, while I still made a few offerings to Neptune in the days to follow, I wasn't hit with overwhelming seasickness. I may not have qualified as an old salt by the end of week one, but I had my sea legs.

Jo and Mr. T, by contrast, seemed to relish our "confused sea state"—sailor speak for waves behaving erratically rather than rhythmically. They hustled about, reefing the mainsail, setting the storm jib, and

---

## IF SOMEONE WAS TO FALL IN OFF ANY BOAT—LET ALONE PLASTIKI—IN THESE CONDITIONS, THEIR TIME IN THIS CHAPTER WOULD BE UP.

---

excitedly yelling orders to us land crabs to ease this line and uncleat that one. An early trial by fire was precisely what the doctor ordered. "The bigger seas and stiffer winds give us the opportunity to push *Plastiki* a little, to really get to know her before venturing too far offshore," explained the ever-chipper Jo.

*Plastiki* made the grade. For the boat to withstand such punishment with all of her parts intact boosted the entire crew's confidence. She was unorthodox in many ways, but this crazy boat might actually make it across the Pacific.

The first week at sea was all about getting accustomed to our new home and new routines. How would I brush my teeth? Where would I pee? What would I have for breakfast? Where on the boat could I find a bit of solitude? It was also about decompressing after the frantic push to get *Plastiki* ready. I slipped into my bunk that first night on water feeling relief, sadness, joy, and

anticipation. For the first time in the three-plus years it took to create *Plastiki*, I wouldn't have to answer people constantly asking, "When do you think you'll be off?"

### CREW VIEW: JO ROYLE

Everyone is a little tired of these conditions that send us flying around the cabin and having to pick the motion of the wave to get the important task of making tea done. One lady seems not to be bothered about getting soaked and thrown around by the big waves—*Plastiki:* She is still trucking along, often at 6 knots, with three reefs and the storm jib.

I feel like a fishwife screeching, "Are you clipped on?" But really, if someone was to fall in off any boat—let alone *Plastiki*—in these conditions, their time in this chapter would be up. Max's life jacket just went off. His face was a picture.

All in all, aside from a few topsy-turvy tummies and the addiction to anything ginger, everyone is, of course, loving it (somewhere just a little deeper down).

..........................

Left behind in San Francisco was the community of devoted Adventure Ecology staff, volunteers, and friends who had helped build *Plastiki* and get the message out. *Plastiki* launched on Saturday, March 20, 2010, amid a lot of hugging and kissing, and more than a few tears. A crowd of well-wishers from the Bay Area, summoned by Twitter and Facebook, gathered at the dock early on that sunny spring morning. Good-byes are always tough, and I secretly had hoped the weather would shut in for a few days to give me more time to spend with family and not feel so rushed. My mom cried; my dog Smudge ran frantically about the boat barking, all very out of character for an otherwise mellow dog. She knew something was up. As Mr. T and Olav pulled in the mooring lines, I called out to the crowd, "See you all in Sydney."

THE HEAVY SEAS OF THE VOYAGE'S FIRST DAYS
BROUGHT ON BOUTS OF SEASICKNESS—BUT BY
THE END OF THE WEEK, DAVID HAD HIS SEA LEGS.

As much as we wanted to sail *Plastiki* beneath the Golden Gate Bridge under her own power, that wouldn't be possible. The wind coming in off the Pacific was simply too strong, and the tide was working against us as well. With an assist by motor launch and accompanied by a small flotilla of kayakers, paddle boarders, small outboards, and sailboats, as well as several helicopters, boats filled with news cameramen, and a larger craft full of close family and friends, *Plastiki* chugged through San Francisco Bay one last time.

Less than twelve hours later, with the open Pacific beckoning and all of the fanfare and best wishes still ringing in our ears, *Plastiki*'s forward progress ground to a less than triumphal halt. Something had a hold of the ship. Vern, Mr. T, and I, the night watch team, could sense a strong ocean current moving against the bottles at waterline, but we were going neither forward nor back.

I shined my flashlight under the boat and found that the line and buoy from a crab pot had snagged around the starboard rudder. Deep in the ocean was a baited trap holding us tight like an anchor. These crab-catching contraptions dotted the coastline like a minefield. Poking at the rope with a pole did no good. Someone would have to go down and cut the line.

FAREWELL LAND—IT'LL BE SEA SEA AND MORE SEA
FOR ALMOST THREE MONTHS—THANKS TO ALL WHO MADE
IT DOWN AND FOR THE ONGOING SUPPORT!
@PLASTIKI 1:04 P.M., MARCH 20, 2010

THE CREW AND FANS GATHERED FOR A TRADITIONAL BLESSING OF
*PLASTIKI*, WHICH ASKED THE GODS FOR PROTECTION. THE WREATH OF
LEAVES REMAINED ON THE SHIP ALL THE WAY TO SYDNEY.

Mr. T didn't hesitate to clamber down through a gap at the edge of the nylon netting strung in lieu of decking between the boat's main beams at the stern. While dangling from the netting with one hand, he attempted to sever the line with a knife held in the other. He couldn't quite reach far enough. And he couldn't squeeze back up through the gap in the netting. Hanging upside down from the netting like a monkey, he was losing strength. To complicate matters, David wasn't tied in or clipped to the safety line. "We're about to lose the co-skipper on our first night," I thought. From the back of the boat, Vern and I grabbed one of David's arms and pulled him to safety.

THERE WILL ALWAYS BE SKEPTICS AND PEOPLE WHO WANT YOU TO FAIL. IMAGINE THE INVECTIVE THAT WOULD HAVE RAINED DOWN ON THOR HEYERDAHL HAD THE INTERNET BEEN AROUND IN 1947.

It was decided that I should try next; since I was six foot four, my reach would be longer. With Jo's insistent warnings about the dangers of falling overboard at the forefront of my mind, I swung under the boat and scooched toward the rudder. The pressure on the crab pot line was immense as I sawed through it. *Boing.* The line snapped, and the boat was free. That buoy rode all the way to Australia, tied to the back of the boat as a souvenir.

### CREW VIEW: JO ROYLE

Olav has his saw out and is working on creating a "secret" out of the piece of wood he brought on board—crazy man. Max is on the helm but has fishing lines out.

David, Mr. T, and Vern are all cozied up in the forepeak catching up on their z's.

Had a good spring-clean after living in a topsy-turvy world for the past couple of days. Olav and I were rewarding ourselves with a coffee, and just as we commented on how beautiful and clean our home was, the coffeepot blew up. *Aarrrggghhh.* Totally messy galley and no coffee—first major drama on board.

Among the catalog of hazards *Plastiki* and her crew took on in crossing the Pacific, crab pots surely wasn't on the list. There was always the possibility the boat's superstructure would suffer mortal damage in heavy weather. Key attachments, held by cashew-sugar epoxy or bolts, might fail. The Seretex material substituting for fiberglass throughout the boat might break apart under the action of sun, salt, and stress. The bottles keeping *Plastiki* afloat might somehow break loose. And then there were the garden-variety dangers inherent to any ocean crossing: squalls, typhoons, falling overboard, running aground on shoals or reefs, and human error. At the marina in Sausalito where *Plastiki* was readied, we were regularly visited by old salts who'd eye the boat up and down and pronounce: "That won't make it out of the bay" or "You hit a typhoon, you're not going to make it."

Online comments to stories about *Plastiki* that ran in *USA Today*, the *New Yorker*, and other news sources in the months before departure were hardly any more charitable. "Coast Guard, get ready," "Sounds like a death trap," and "Don't spend a penny rescuing this guy when his boat falls apart" were pretty typical. My attitude is that there will always be skeptics and people who want you to fail. If you worry about failure, you're not going to get anything done in this life. With *Plastiki*, we assembled a team of the best people, used the best materials possible, mitigated risk in the construction as much as we could, and we did something that was going to inspire people whether we made it to Sydney or not. If all else failed, we had the inflatable emergency raft and EPIRB radio distress beacon to fall back on.

Imagine the invective that would have rained down on Thor Heyerdahl over his plan to sail the Pacific on a raft of balsa logs lashed together with hemp rope had the Internet been around in 1947. Heyerdahl wasn't without his critics. Nearly everyone who heard of his plan or saw *Kon-Tiki* under construction was quite sure he was mad or had a death wish, or both. But Heyerdahl believed strongly in his renegade theory that the inhabitants of Polynesia were descended not from Indonesians or Australian Aborigines, as generally accepted, but rather from pre-Incan people who migrated in bulky rafts from South America, borne westward some 4,300 miles by ocean currents and the trade winds.

### CREW VIEW: MAX JOURDAN
..........................

Emerging into the strange night for the 4 A.M. watch, you venture to the deck's edge and fumble with layers and zips as you lean over the edge to relieve yourself. Jo casually mentions, "Most sailors who are lost at sea are found with their tackle out."

There's a full moon tonight. Mesmerizing, huge, white, round, and dead ahead. Its reflected light forms a giant silver *V* over the water.

The hours flash by, and looking at the boat's wake you realize dawn is approaching. Tonight the ocean is iridescent purple, with lines of orange and blue edging the sky. Olav said, "Look at the moon dropping into the water," but you can't take your gaze away from what's approaching from behind. The entire sky is humming as light from the atomic sun arcs through the atmosphere. Overwhelmed, you just want to scream and howl and rage with the beauty of it all, but the rest of the crew is already asleep.

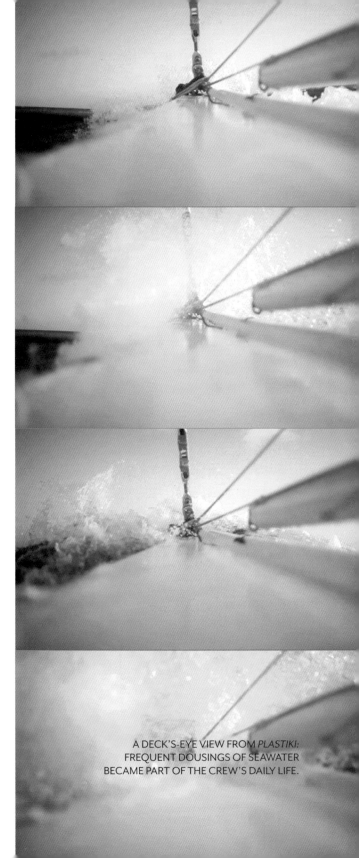

A DECK'S-EYE VIEW FROM *PLASTIKI*: FREQUENT DOUSINGS OF SEAWATER BECAME PART OF THE CREW'S DAILY LIFE.

Heyerdahl's humble raft made it, crash-landing after 101 days at sea onto the reef at Raroia in the Tuamotu Islands; his theory, ultimately, did not. Like *Kon-Tiki*, *Plastiki* also is about challenging assumptions. Right now, society is accustomed to regarding plastic as a valueless and ultimately disposable material. Out of a substance that lasts for thousands of years, we make packaging and products designed to be used for just ten minutes—and oftentimes less than that. The tragic dimensions of that throwaway mind-set are seen in our oceans—and in their inhabitants—filling up with plastic. We can change that.

Plastic itself isn't to blame. Plastic's amazing qualities made possible huge advances in medicine, technology, entertainment, transportation, and pretty much every facet of modern life. The problem is our inability to understand that trashing plastic at the end of its useful life is a design flaw.

In natural systems, garbage doesn't exist. Dung and death yield vital nutrients that are soon metabolized by other organisms in an endless cycle of buildup and breakdown, construction and destruction. By creating value for postconsumer plastics, we can change the perception of plastic from that of garbage to valuable commodity. When waste streams yield to closed-loop materials cycles in which a plastic bottle is "upcycled" back into a plastic bottle again, and when plastic products and packaging are designed from the outset with their end of use in mind, then we can slow and perhaps even reverse the alarming environmental damage occurring around the planet due to plastic pollution. We just need curiosity, imagination, and time to innovate in order to stop these human fingerprints.

SAILING DUTIES WERE SHARED AMONG ALL THE CREW; HERE, OLAV HOLDS THE TILLER DURING *PLASTIKI'S* FIRST DAYS ON THE PACIFIC.

### CREW VIEW: JO ROYLE

It is sleepyheads all around on *Plastiki* tonight. At one point when we were turning in circles due to lack of wind, we did consider dropping all the sails and going for a mammoth sleep. Three hours at a time, really!? Whose idea was that? By the time you change watch, do any moves that involve everyone being on deck, make the "on watch" a cup of tea, check the navigation, and get the million layers of clothes off, you really only get two and a half hours of sleep, max. Okay, stopping the whining. Life out here is great, really.

Tonight has been slow going. Everyone has done a brilliant job of keeping their cool as helming the boat downwind in very light winds takes the patience of an angel to avoid an accidental jibe. Yesterday afternoon we had the big downwind spinnaker up, trucking along. No one could get Mr. T off the helm.

.........................

As a class of oceangoing sailing vessels, multihulls enjoy a reputation for being fast and stable. A typical oceangoing twin-hull, or catamaran, can attain speeds of 20 knots or better. *USA-17*, the trimaran challenger in the 2010 America's Cup, and *Alinghi 5*, the catamaran defender, hit top speeds in excess of 30 knots (35 miles per hour) in their duels. *Plastiki* might have shared the same genetics as those craft but certainly not their fleetness. Our top speed in the first leg of the journey

was 7.8 knots, a speed that made Jo uncomfortable from the force of the waves on the bottles and the vibrating of the cables and wires that secured the masts. More often than not, *Plastiki* puttered along at 3 knots or less. What's 3 knots like? Go outside and walk at a brisk pace. Continue till Australia.

Speed was not a top priority when designing *Plastiki*. Had it been, we would have sheathed the plastic bottles packed into the hulls in some sort of translucent plastic skin. Doing so would have significantly diminished drag and created more rigidity in the boat's structure. It also would have been the easy route. My directive to designer Andy Dovell had been to make the bottles visible *and* functional. If we sacrificed speed to play up the iconic stature of the bottles, then who cared? Well, one person in particular: Vern. Vern's wife, Melinda, was pregnant with their first child. The due date was April 23. When Vern enlisted to film the journey, the launch date was set for December 2009. Had we left then, Vern would have been home in Long Beach before the birth with room to spare.

However, production delays kept pushing the departure date, putting Vern in a tighter and tighter bind. "At what point do I say 'No'?" he wondered aloud in one of our many conversations on the topic. With March 20 set as a firm launch date from Sausalito, we agreed that Vern would chronicle the first leg of the journey and then fly back from wherever we made landfall to be with his wife. He'd be cutting it close. Melinda was incredibly understanding and supportive of his dilemma. "It is what it is," she told Vern. "Enjoy yourself and do your job."

Then the best laid plans ran into the reality of what a slow sailor *Plastiki* turned out to be. Two weeks into the trip, it was plain that we were behind schedule. Vern's spirits rose and fell with the wind speed. The pressure he was under was palpable, and as the calendar turned, that pressure kept building and transferred to the rest

EVERYDAY LIFE ON BOARD, CLOCKWISE FROM TOP LEFT: A POWER SYSTEM CHECK; OCCASIONAL WARM SHOWERS; OPEN-AIR YOGA ON CUSTOM *PLASTIKI* YOGA MATS; AND ALWAYS BEING SURE TO CLIP IN LOOSE OBJECTS—AND *PLASTIKI*'S SAILORS.

# CREW PROFILE: DAVID DE ROTHSCHILD

Greenland. Antarctica. Amazonian Ecuador. David's passion and commitment to the environment have sent him on adventures to some of the world's most remote and fragile regions, alerting the world to pressing issues and their solutions. In 2005, he founded Adventure Ecology to inspire individuals, communities, and businesses to start moving toward a smarter, more sustainable "Planet 2.0" way of living. He has been named a National Geographic Society "Emerging Explorer" and a United Nations Environment Programme "Climate Hero."

### WHAT ACCOUNTS FOR YOUR WANDERLUST?

Being a naturally curious and hyperactive person means I'm always keen to keep moving and exploring.

### DID YOU SUFFER "NATURE DEFICIT DISORDER" AS A KID?

No, I was bathed in nature as a child. I wanted to spend every waking hour outside. As soon as I was dragged inside, I would cause lots of trouble to get sent outside.

### FAVORITE CHILDHOOD MEMORY OF THE OUTDOORS?

Most of my younger years were spent riding horses and living on a farm. I spent hours building camps in haystacks and seeing if I could jump off the top of them without hurting myself. It always hurt.

### WORST TROUBLE YOU GOT INTO AS A KID?

When I was ten years old, I foraged these pods that look like sugar snap peas to provide food for my campmates. It turns out the pods were from a tree called a laburnum and highly poisonous. I sent myself and eight other students to the hospital to have our stomachs pumped.

### WHAT DID YOU WANT TO BE WHEN YOU GREW UP?

I was pretty set on being a jockey. Then I grew.

### MOTTO YOU LIVE BY?

"Nobody is as smart as everybody."

### WHAT TURNED YOU INTO AN ENVIRO?

During my late teens, I became deeply interested in the idea that you are what you eat and what you breathe. This lead me to follow an education in natural medicine, which very quickly allowed me to explore the connections between health and the environment. That unlocked my curiosity in environmentalism.

### PLASTIC BOTTLES ASIDE, GOT ANY OTHER ENVIRONMENTAL PEEVES?

Humanity's general lack of regard for how nature plays a pivotal role in every element of our daily activities, yet we still treat it with such little respect and care. Oh, and hotels that wrap Styrofoam cups in plastic.

### "ECO-ADVENTURER" SOUNDS LIKE A FUN JOB TITLE. EVER HELD A DESK JOB?

I was a scooter salesman at age eighteen, and it bored me silly. But I got a free scooter.

### WHAT GOT YOU HOOKED ON BIG-TIME ADVENTURE?

Traversing Antarctica in 2004. The scale, honesty, and rawness of that adventure were more than enough to get me hooked.

## THERE WAS ANOTHER SOURCE OF CONCERN GROWING WITH EACH DAY WE DROPPED OFF SCHEDULE. OUR FRESHWATER WAS RUNNING OUT.

of the team. Try as we might to roll with whatever the Pacific Ocean brought us each day, everyone was painfully aware of Vern's deadline.

### CREW VIEW: VERN MOEN

It might sound bizarre, but I have quite a unique relationship with our spinnaker. My wife is eight months pregnant with our first child, due on April 23. The estimated time from San Francisco to the Line Islands (where I'm scheduled to get off *Plastiki*) is approximately thirty days.

Obviously, this isn't an ideal situation for me, but there are times when two amazing, once-in-a-lifetime opportunities happen simultaneously. Enter the spinnaker. Two days ago we were stuck with little to no wind and moving at a paltry 1.5 knots!

The spinnaker went up and instantly we were at 6 knots. So for me the spinnaker is a symbol of hope and happiness. Potential baby name: Spinnaker Moen. We'll see how it works out.

....................

There was another source of concern growing with each day we dropped off schedule. Our freshwater was running out. We had departed Sausalito with enough water to last fifty days. Jo and David had calculated that supply based on an old sailor's rule of thumb of 3 liters per person per day. Not much when you consider our

daily ration would have to suffice for drinking, cooking, brushing teeth, and bathing. We expected to supplement our stores with rainfall captured from the boat's cleverly designed roof, but the few brief rain showers we'd encountered did little good. What hadn't been factored in was the orgy of water use we indulged in during our first ten days at sea. Jo informed us that starting immediately we were back on a strict daily personal ration of three liters. Without a pickup in speed or an end to the drought, Jo said she'd cut us back to two liters.

I've never questioned Jo's judgment on anything but this one issue of how much drinking water to carry. On the three-day sea trial in February, we had averaged six liters of personal consumption each day. Jo and David explained away that high level of use as a result of several of us being seasick, which we presumably wouldn't be—at least for very long—on the actual journey. I argued for taking along more water, since I'd rather have too much than too little. However, at two pounds per liter, water is heavy. Jo's point was that extra water would slow down an already slow vessel. Now, mid-ocean, I was upset with myself that I hadn't been more insistent.

As a side note, I had received an odd warning of a possible water crisis months back while still in Sausalito. Out of the blue I received a phone call from a former girlfriend, a psychic named Amaryllis. We hadn't spo-

MASSIVE MASSIVE WAVES ALL OVER THE PLACE
SHE IS STANDING UP WELL THOUGH :)
@DREXPLORE 5:04 P.M., MARCH 23, 2010

DAVID THOMSON LIKED TO SPEND HIS NIGHT WATCH
WITH CHOCOLATES AND A BOOK. TOGETHER, THE
CREW READ THIRTY-TWO BOOKS AND ATE 1,175
CHOCOLATE BARS.

*PLASTIKI*'S FIRST FISH—A YELLOWFIN TUNA BROUGHT IN BY MAX—FED US HAPPILY FOR DAYS. IT TURNED OUT TO BE ONE OF ONLY THREE FISH CAUGHT DURING THE ENTIRE VOYAGE.

Could you live without plastic? Beth Terry of Oakland, California, gave it a try. Her lifestyle experiment, chronicled on the blog fakeplasticfish.com, demonstrates how pervasive plastic is in our lives, as well as just how quickly we might cut our use of it down to size.

Begun in July 2007 and recorded with the precision of an accountant (which Beth is in real life), her effort to reduce the amount of discarded plastic has achieved real success. From an initial monthly tally of 242 pieces of plastic weighing 3 pounds, she pared down her waste to an all-time low of 16 pieces weighing a mere 4.7 ounces in October 2009.

After knocking out obvious sources of plastic by avoiding frozen prepared meals, shopping with reusable bags, and buying rice, cereal, and other basics from bulk bins at Whole Foods, Beth's ensuing cuts took real ingenuity. She washes her hair with diluted baking soda (ratio of 1 tablespoon to 1 cup of water) and rinses with diluted apple cider vinegar (same ratio), bakes her own energy bars, totes a drinking glass to picnics, and finds used durable plastic goods like computers and dishwashers on Craigslist and Freecycle. "There's so much plastic around, I feel like we should use what's already here," says Beth.

ken to or seen each other in years. "You haven't gone on your trip yet, have you?" she asked. I assured her I hadn't. "Oh, thank goodness. I had this premonition, and you need to be really careful with dehydration on the trip. I see dehydration. Take along some electrolytes," she said.

I doubted we were in danger of reenacting "The Rime of the Ancient Mariner," but when the daytime temperature hovers in the 90s, the tropical sun beats down, and salt is everywhere—even in the jerky, nuts, porridge, and curry you eat—then the desire to drink becomes all-consuming. It played on my mind a lot. In a mixed blessing, the water pumped up out of the hold tasted horrible. Stored in 400-liter bladders, it tasted, ironically, like plastic. For Vern, for me, for everyone, checking the boat's navigation program on the computer became a preoccupation. It projected that, at a speed of 4.3 knots, we would arrive on Christmas Island in the Line Islands in precisely twelve days. At 2 knots, we wouldn't get there for twenty days—too late for Vern and a major problem for the rest of us. Landfall couldn't come soon enough.

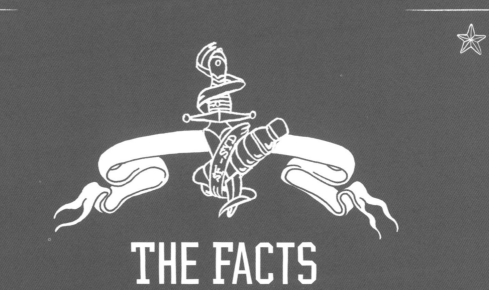

# THE FACTS

EACH YEAR, PLASTIC LITTER IN THE OCEANS
KILLS 100,000 TURTLES, DOLPHINS, WHALES,
AND OTHER MARINE MAMMALS—
AND 1 MILLION SEABIRDS.

OUR CONSUMPTION OF FRESHWATER
MULTIPLIED SIX TIMES IN THE
TWENTIETH CENTURY—TWICE THE RATE
OF POPULATION GROWTH.

# POP STARS ARE FINE, BUT CELEBRATE THOSE WHO ARE DOWN TO-EARTH

### BY PHILIPPE COUSTEAU

I was at the grocery store the other day, minding my own business, when I noticed the woman in front of me pull out a large cloth reusable sack at the checkout aisle.

"Progress!" I thought to myself with satisfaction. Then I watched in horror as she first placed her purchases into several plastic bags and then placed those into the reusable bag.

As I walked out of the store, I realized two things: The good news is that we are making progress (she had a reusable bag); the bad news is that we clearly have a long way to go.

First let's explore the good news.

I believe it is no small thing that I am contributing this piece to a global adventure like *Plastiki,* which is getting attention on an international level from the likes of traditional media such as CNN as well as Web sites and other green networks—none of which would have been conceivable just a decade ago.

You see, for most of the twentieth century, environmentalists were often seen as granola-eating hippies living on communes, and being green was perceived as a passing fancy sulking on the fringes of society. While that has certainly changed, as the woman at the grocery store reminded me, we still have an uphill battle ahead of us.

Now the bad news.

In the United States the public is almost evenly split between those who think climate change is real and those who do not. Despite the fact that an overwhelming amount of science supports the climate change reality, we are rarely a science-driven society either politically or socially. Instead it seems we regularly prefer pithy sound bites that support our world view rather than intelligent arguments that challenge us to learn and expand our understanding—and the media is no different.

One morning recently I picked up a major national newspaper, and as I flipped to the metro section I was greeted by a large picture of a koi fish. The cover story was about the National Arboretum in Washington, D.C., and how they were conducting their annual koi fish auction.

It wasn't until I glanced down at the article that was unceremoniously squeezed beneath extensive coverage of a fish sale at the bottom of the page that I found what I was looking for: a brief story covering one of the most incredible achievements of humankind.

That weekend, in addition to being the time when a national institution auctioned off oversize goldfish, was also when we celebrated the fiftieth anniversary of the *Trieste* descending to the bottom of Challenger Deep, the deepest point on earth 7 miles beneath the shiny waves of the Pacific Ocean.

Only two men have ever gone that deep in the history of all humanity, and that was fifty years ago! Don Walsh and Jacques Piccard both risked their lives to descend that deep, and only the former is still alive.

More men have landed on the Moon than have reached the deepest part of our own planet, and despite the progress I mentioned earlier, we are still struggling to recognize that this planet and all its wonder should be valued above all else.

Pop stars and sports figures are fine, but we should equally value those who continue to fight for a more just, enlightened, and hopeful future.

Teachers, scientists, explorers, and the like are heroes who walk among us every day and deserve more than a passing mention at the bottom of the newspaper.

That is why *Plastiki* is so important in my opinion; it reminds us that nature is both to be explored and revered, but that it is also a fragile victim of our greed and stupidity.

As *Plastiki* sails through an ocean of trash, we should all be ashamed of what we have done to this planet and what we have condemned our children to live with.

I hope that if *Plastiki* inspires us to do anything, it is to think a little bit more about the choices we make and, at the very least, cut out the plastic bags.

...

*Philippe Cousteau, grandson of famed oceanographer Jacques Cousteau, is president of EarthEcho International, which grooms the next generation of ocean champions.*

# 4

POLYMERS ARE FOREVER

THERE IS NO "AWAY" FOR PLASTIC WASTE: IT LASTS
FOREVER, MUCH OF IT SWIRLING IN OUR OCEANS'
"GARBAGE PATCHES." *PLASTIKI* REPRESENTS ONE
WAY TOWARD A BETTER, LESS-PLASTIC FUTURE.

I was taking the ferry from the island of Savaii back to Upolu after doing some sightseeing. Savaii, like Upolu, is immaculate. Every street and sidewalk is laid out perfectly, every hedge is trimmed, and median strips are crisply mowed. People in every village take evident pride in the appearance of their homes. I didn't see a piece of trash anywhere. Recycling programs are very advanced in Samoa, and biodegradable plastic bags are mandatory. Okay, back to the ferry. It was a beautiful tropical afternoon, and sitting across from me on the deck of the ferry were three generations of a family: a fragile grandmother, her middle-aged daughter, and a young grandson and granddaughter. They were talking amiably in their native Samoan, when the older woman finished off the water she was holding and threw the bottle straight over the railing into the ocean. Five minutes later, her daughter did exactly the same thing.

I practically fell out of my seat. There isn't a chance either woman would have littered back home in their spotless village. They would have done the right thing and put their bottles in a bin. I didn't confront the women, and the language barrier wouldn't have helped my cause. I can only surmise their attitude must be, "It's not my backyard, and anyway it's a big ocean. Those bottles will go somewhere else." But that's just it; there is no such place as "away." Everything in the water is connected.

For the sake of the oceans and for our own sake, we have to stop regarding plastic as a throwaway. Certain dumb uses of plastic should be curtailed right away, like the ubiquitous plastic shopping bag and Styrofoam. Practical alternatives for them already exist. We also have to make collecting and reusing every type of plastic easier. When supplies of recycled plastic become steady and predictable, we will set in motion a virtuous cycle in which plastics have more value, so recycling rates go higher still. All of a sudden, entrepreneurship will flow through the supply chain of plastics, and there's no end to where that can lead.

Imagine the journey of your typical, everyday water bottle. An empty bottle of Dasani mistakenly left on top of a car by its owner bounces to the side of Grand View Drive in Los Angeles. A strong winter storm has rolled in

# PLASTIC 101

FOR EVERY LITRE OF WATER POURED INTO A BOTTLE

ANOTHER 2 LITRES ARE USED IN ITS MANUFACTURE

20% OF THE SPACE IN YOUR BIN IS TAKEN UP WITH OLD PLASTIC — ONLY 7% BY WEIGHT

ENOUGH OIL TO FUEL 100,000 CARS TO MAKE A YEAR'S WORTH OF PLASTIC WATER BOTTLES IN NORTH AMERICA ALONE

230 MILLION TONNES OF PLASTIC ARE CONSUMED BY THE WORLD EVERY YEAR

THE UK PLASTICS INDUSTRY IS WORTH

MORE THAN 90% OF PLASTICS ARE NOT RECYCLED

WE RECYCLE LESS THAN 10% OF PLASTICS IN THE UK

£17.5 BILLION + EMPLOYS 220,000

SCIENTISTS ESTIMATE THAT ONE MILLION SEA BIRDS + 100,000 MARINE MAMMALS AND SEA TURTLES DIE FROM PLASTIC POLLUTION EVERY YEAR

TOTAL MARINE POLLUTION IS 60-80% PLASTIC MATERIALS

15 BILLION POUNDS OF PLASTIC ARE PRODUCED IN THE US EVERY YEAR — ONLY 1 BILLION ARE RECYCLED

200 BILLION LITRES OF BOTTLED WATER CONSUMED PER YEAR

PLASTIC MATERIALS CONSTITUTE AS MUCH AS 90-95% OF ALL MARINE DEBRIS

27 million TONNES

4/5 BOTTLES END UP IN A LANDFILL

IF EVERYONE IN NYC GAVE UP WATER BOTTLES FOR...

ONE WEEK SAVE 24 MILLION

ONE MONTH SAVE 112 MILLION

ONE YEAR SAVE 1328 BILLION

4% OF ALL THE OIL WE EXTRACT IS TURNED INTO PLASTICS

IS BURNED TO FUEL THE PROCESS

LARGE FLOATING DEBRIS IS RARE IN THE
GARBAGE PATCH. THE VAST MAJORITY OF
PLASTIC WASTE ERODES INTO TINY PARTICLES
SUSPENDED IN THE WATER.

from the Pacific, dousing the city with 2 inches of much-needed rain. Street runoff fills the gutter and sends the sealed bottle, a blue-tinged, perfectly buoyant cell of air, coasting downhill. At a storm drain, the bottle hesitates before disappearing from sight. Through a series of drainpipes, the bottle emerges into the light just as it goes airborne and plops into a concrete channel known as the Los Angeles River.

Dry for half the year, the river today is a rain-swollen brown torrent that rides high on the embankment walls. In a matter of hours, the Dasani bottle has bobbed past downtown skyscrapers, under I-10, through Compton, and is flushed into Los Angeles Harbor at Long Beach.

THE EXACT AMOUNT OF PLASTIC ENTERING THE PACIFIC OCEAN IS UNKNOWN, AND MAY BE UNKNOWABLE. BUT WHAT IS CERTAIN IS THAT THE GARBAGE PATCH HAS GROWN IN SIZE, AND SO HAS THE DENSITY OF PLASTIC WITHIN ITS VORTEX.

Carried by the surge of floodwater, the bottle breaches the tidal zone and is soon riding in the open ocean. As days and weeks go by, the bottle, looking good as new, drifts south on the cold California Current toward San Diego and then beyond Cabo San Lucas at the tip of Baja.

On a timescale measured in years, the cast-off bottle will meander the North Pacific in a clockwise spiral, nearly reaching Japan before sweeping back to the east. In a zone between Hawaii and California marked by abnormally weak winds and persistent heat and sunshine, the water bottle's grand tour will effectively end. It will have entered the Great Pacific Garbage Patch, a final resting place for floating rubbish. Once in the grips of the garbage patch—an immense whirlpool powered

by the stack of high-pressure atmosphere above it—the Dasani bottle will never escape.

Our wandering water bottle was not alone in traveling to the garbage patch. When the Los Angeles River flows, 1 ton of assorted bottles, shopping bags, Styrofoam, straws, swizzle sticks, lighters, caps, traffic cones, and other plastic objects enters the Pacific each and every day on average. Add to that the plastic discharge from the San Gabriel River—which similarly channels through L.A. to the ocean—and the plastic outflow from the San Joaquin and Sacramento rivers, which drain most of central and northern California. Add to that the floating effluent of the Pacific Northwest's mighty Columbia, Vietnam's Mekong, China's Yellow, Yangtze, and Pearl rivers, and the outwash from every street, parking lot, and misplaced landfill in Manila, Seoul, Taipei, and Tokyo. Adding to the mess, fishing fleets, freighters, and cruise ships toss their garbage directly into the ocean.

The exact amount of plastic entering the Pacific Ocean is unknown, and may be unknowable. But what is certain is that the garbage patch is growing in size and in the density of plastic within its vortex. What had been two distinct garbage patches as recently as a decade ago—a western patch between Japan and Hawaii, and an eastern patch between California and Hawaii—have converged. Comprehending the scale of the Great Pacific Garbage Patch strains the imagination. East to west, it sprawls across an area that begins roughly 200 miles off the California coast and runs nearly to China. North to south it stretches from the 40th parallel to the 20th, or the equivalent distance from New York City to Haiti.

Like a vast amoeba, the Great Pacific Garbage Patch shifts and contorts with the seasons and changing weather patterns, slopping south in the winter and oozing north in summer. Estimates of its size become outdated almost as soon as they go into print. From being "twice the size of Texas" ten years

# THE FIVE GYRES

ALTHOUGH NOT WIDELY DISCUSSED THERE ARE IN FACT 5 MAIN GYRES IN THE WORLD'S OCEANS AND SEVERAL SMALLER GYRES THROUGHOUT ALASKA AND ANTARCTICA. THE MOST COMMONLY DISCUSSED GYRE IS THE NORTH PACIFIC GYRE, KNOWN AS THE GARBAGE PATCH DUE TO THE MASS OF MARINE DEBRIS THAT HAS COLLECTED THERE.

Albatross fly huge distances to feed their young a deadly diet of plastic pellets.

A sea turtle found dead in Hawaii had over a 1000 pieces of plastic in its stomach and intestines.

Plastic fragments outnumber zoo plankton 40 to 1.

There are six pounds of plastic for every pound of algae.

THE NORTH PACIFIC GARBAGE PATCH IS TWICE THE SIZE OF TEXAS – APX 10,000,000 SQ NAUTICAL MILES (34,000,000 SQ KILOMETRES)

IT IS THE LARGEST GYRE ON EARTH AND CONTAINS ROUGHLY 3.5 MILLION TONS OF TRASH.

Plastic particles are pushed gently in a slow moving spiral towards the centre.

EVERY OCEAN SAMPLE TEST CONDUCTED PRODUCED SOME FORM OF PLASTIC WASTE IN THE NORTH ATLANTIC.

107 plastic pieces were found in 1 sq foot on a southern beach in Bermuda.

61% of the plastic in the ocean is less than a mm.

**NORTH PACIFIC GYRE**

**NORTH ATLANTIC GYRE**

The plastics act as a sort of 'chemical sponge'. They contain Persistent Organic Pollutants (POPs). Animals eating these pieces of plastic debris will also be taking in highly toxic pollutants.

## A GYRE

A gyre is a place where currents meet and form a whirl pool type system - this forms a meeting place for ocean debris. Millions of tiny and large pieces of plastics accumulate here; due to the currents they remain trapped here, breaking down over time to become smaller and smaller pieces of plastic until they eventually become plastic dust.

This 'dust' will never go away but will instead stay in the ocean accumulating toxins and working its way into the food chain as more animals digest these invisible and dangerous items of plastic waste.

SUNLIGHT AND WAVE ACTION CAUSE THESE FLOATING PLASTICS TO FRAGMENT, BREAKING INTO SMALLER PARTICLES, BUT NEVER COMPLETELY DISAPPEARING.

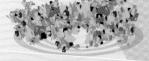

**SOUTH PACIFIC GYRE**

**SOUTH ATLANTIC GYRE**

1 million sea birds & 100,000 mammals & sea turtles die from plastic pollution every year.

Studies have found that Fulmars have an average of 30 pieces of plastic in their stomachs.

Toxic chemicals enter the food chain via plastics.

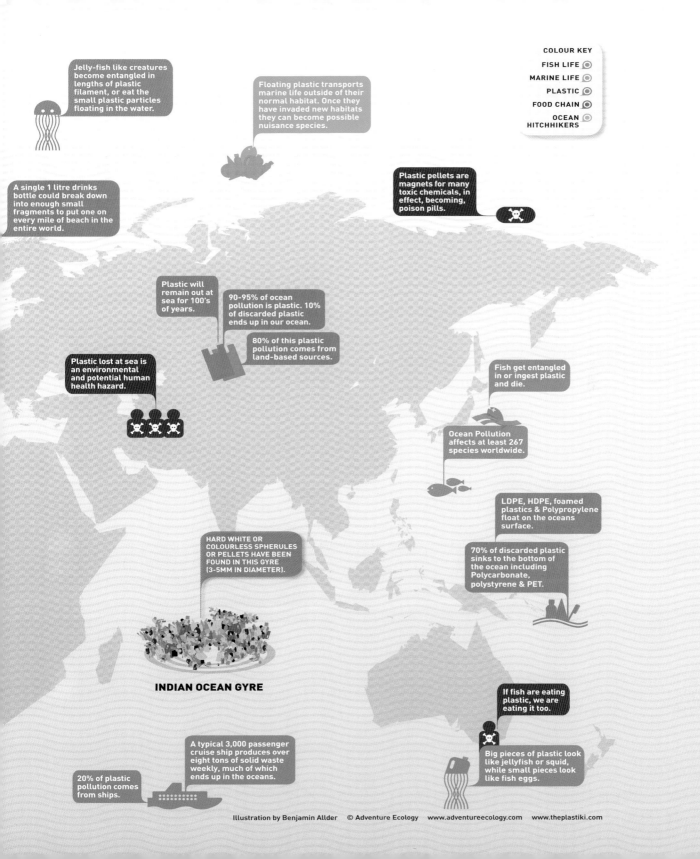

## GREAT MOMENTS IN PLASTIC HISTORY

If it seems like plastic is everywhere, that's because it is. How did we get to this synthetic state?

1869 Celluloid, a plastic made of natural materials, debuts. Elephants everywhere cheer: Ivory billiard balls are now made from the material.

1907 Leo Baekeland mistakenly creates the first synthetic polymer. Dubbed "Bakelite," it's still used today in electronics and aerospace.

1930 Injection molding speeds output of windup chattering teeth and other plastic essentials.

1938 Nylon stockings introduced. First run occurs five minutes later.

1948 First Tupperware Party held.

1953 Plastic wrap unveiled as food keeper, then thirty years later as bodywear by Cher.

1962 Hula hoops sweep the nation: Plastic playtime begins.

1965 The first polystyrene packing peanut blows into a gutter.

1975 Plastic soda containers kill off deposit-return bottling, a great leap in garbage production.

1977 John Travolta popularizes polyester leisure suits in *Saturday Night Fever*.

1977 Perrier launches its $5 million marketing campaign for bottled water. Tap water is suddenly uncool.

1990 McDonald's discontinues foam clamshell containers after uproar.

2005 The FDA reapproves silicone breast implants after thirteen-year ban.

ago, the patch may now cover an area twice the size of the United States.

"The amount of plastic entering the gyre is going up exponentially," says Charles Moore, the man credited with bringing the trashing of the oceans to public awareness. Moore is director of the Algalita Marine Research

### LIKE A VAST AMOEBA, THE GREAT PACIFIC GARBAGE PATCH SHIFTS AND CONTORTS WITH THE SEASONS AND CHANGING WEATHER PATTERNS.

Foundation, an organization he formed in 1999 on the heels of an eye-opening ocean voyage. Moore was returning to Long Beach, California, in his catamaran *Alguita* after competing in the Transpacific Yacht Race from Los Angeles to Honolulu, when he had the notion to sail under motor power through a windless area that sailors usually skirt around. He couldn't get over the amount of plastic found floating in this dead zone. "The water we motored through was full of shampoo bottles, bottle caps, fishing nets. This went on without letup for days," he says.

Moore returned to the garbage patch in 2000 equipped with a trawling net in an attempt to determine the size of the debris zone and the amount of plastic in it. "I thought I'd be looking for larger pieces of plastic, but it turns out that's not the real story. The water is filled with small pellets of plastic, like confetti. We were collecting six times as much plastic as we were zooplankton," he says. Depending on their specific gravity and whether algae, barnacles, or some other sea life has hitched a ride, these plastic particles float in soupy suspension to a depth of 100 feet.

Moore finds the term *garbage patch* a little too

# ONE WORD! PLASTICS

WE ARE NOW LITERALLY SWIMMING IN A SEA OF PLASTICS! ALMOST EVERYTHING YOU EAT, WEAR, CARRY, SLEEP AND WASH WITH IS PROBABLY FROM THIS FAMILY OF 7! BUT HAVE YOU EVER WONDERED WHAT THOSE FUNNY LITTLE NUMBERS STAND FOR? URRMMM NO! ITS NOT A GAME OF BINGO! THAT'S WHY WE HAVE CREATED THIS EASY REFERENCE GUIDE, SO NOT ONLY CAN YOU NOW IMPRESS YOUR FRIENDS AND FAMILY BY PRETENDING TO BE A POLYMER SCIENTIST BUT NOW YOU WILL KNOW EXACTLY HOW TO SEPARATE ALL YOUR PLASTICS FOR RECYCLING - LEAVING ONE LESS PLASTIC CONTAINER, BOTTLE OR BAG FLOATING AROUND IN OUR NATURAL WORLD!

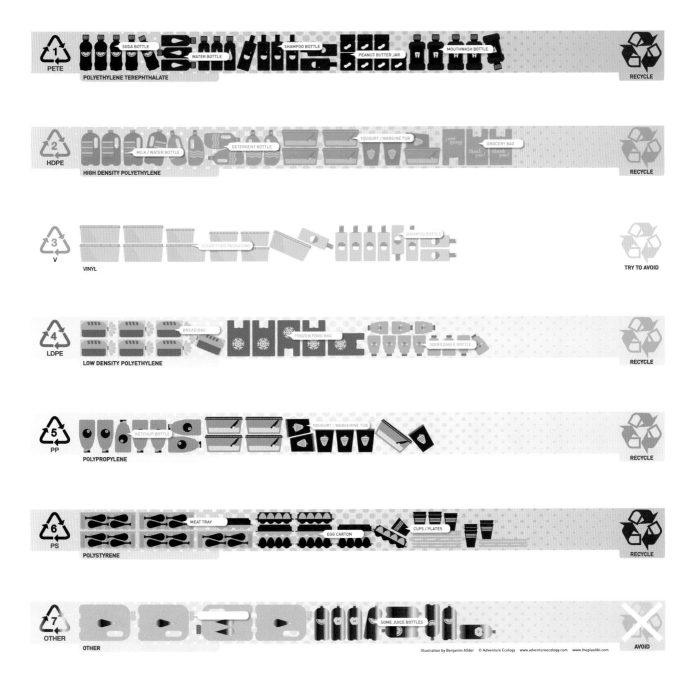

**1 PETE** — POLYETHYLENE TEREPHTHALATE — SODA BOTTLE, WATER BOTTLE, SHAMPOO BOTTLE, PEANUT BUTTER JAR, MOUTHWASH BOTTLE — RECYCLE

**2 HDPE** — HIGH DENSITY POLYETHYLENE — MILK / WATER BOTTLE, DETERGENT BOTTLE, YOUGURT / MARGINE TUB, GROCERY BAG — RECYCLE

**3 V** — VINYL — CLEAR FOOD PACKAGING, SHAMPOO BOTTLE — TRY TO AVOID

**4 LDPE** — LOW DENSITY POLYETHYLENE — BREAD BAG, FROZEN FOOD BAG, SQUEEZABLE BOTTLE — RECYCLE

**5 PP** — POLYPROPYLENE — KETCHUP BOTTLE, YOUGURT / MARGERINE TUB — RECYCLE

**6 PS** — POLYSTYRENE — MEAT TRAY, EGG CARTON, CUPS / PLATES — RECYCLE

**7 OTHER** — OTHER — SOME JUICE BOTTLES — AVOID

Illustration by Benjamin Allder   © Adventure Ecology   www.adventureecology.com   www.theplastiki.com

cute and also inadequate in expressing the extent of the problem in the Pacific, conveying as it does the impression of a pumpkin patch or floating island with defined borders. He favors *accumulation zone*. On multiple trips back to the gyre using trawls with netting as fine as 1 mm, Moore and his research teams have yet to find a boundary to the accumulation zone.

EVEN OUTSIDE KNOWN ACCUMULATION ZONES, PLASTIC IS PRESENT AT WORRISOME CONCENTRATIONS. ON PLASTIKI, WE FOUND THIS TO BE TRUE AS WE SAILED WELL SOUTH OF THE GARBAGE PATCH.

The closer Moore's Algalita Marine Research Foundation and others study the problem of marine plastic debris, the more widespread it reveals itself to be. Anywhere in our oceans where currents form a gyre, you'll find a buildup of plastics.

Moore now estimates there are nine accumulation zones of heavy plastic concentration worldwide. Every ocean has one. At the 2010 Ocean Sciences meeting, two independent teams of researchers presented evidence of a mammoth garbage patch caught in the North Atlantic Subtropic Convergence Zone between Bermuda and the Azores Islands. By some estimates, more than 100 million tons of plastic now clog our oceans, some of it decades old.

For beachgoers the world over, plastic debris is a visual blight. Landmasses that end up in the path of the rotating gyres are hit hardest. The nineteen islands of the Hawaiian archipelago, including Midway Atoll, regularly get dumped on, with some beaches buried beneath several feet of trash. Other beaches are riddled with "plastic sand," granular pieces of plastic that are impossible to clean up.

For wild creatures from whales to krill, the effects of ocean-borne plastics are ravaging. Animals become entangled or strangled by plastic sheeting, six-pack holders, and "ghost nets"—lost nets adrift in the ocean. Sea turtles ingest plastic bags, mistaking them for jellyfish; plankton sweep in tiny plastic pellets; and dead whales have been autopsied with a disturbing variety of plastic objects caught in their stomachs.

The saddest evidence of plastic's effect on animals has to be pictures of dead birds at the edge of the garbage patch. Midway Atoll is a thousand miles from the nearest city yet is often awash in plastic trash, and for the long-distance Laysan albatross that nests there, it's within range of the Great Pacific Garbage Patch. The photos from Midway Atoll show the skeletons of albatross chicks surrounding small piles of plastic objects that had clogged their stomachs. You can't look at the photos without your heart being wrenched. Albatrosses scour the ocean surface for hundreds of miles looking for fish and squid on the surface to feed their young. In the hunt, they scoop up floating syringes, clothespins, toy soldiers, bottle caps, golf tees, and other plastics, which they confuse for edibles. They then regurgitate their find to feed their chicks. Of the estimated 500,000 Laysan albatross chicks born on Midway each year, an estimated 30 to 40 percent die from dehydration, starvation, and other complications due to gullets and bellies filled with plastic.

Even well outside known accumulation zones, plastic is present at worrisome concentrations. On *Plastiki*, we found this to be true as we sailed for the Line Islands well south of the garbage patch. (News stories about *Plastiki* often reported our itinerary would take us through the garbage patch, but that was never a realistic option simply because you can't sail where there is no wind.) Every day, we saw bits of trash floating past: plastic bottles, bags, jerricans, a garden plant tray, wrappers, and a 3-foot-square white PVC tray riding in the

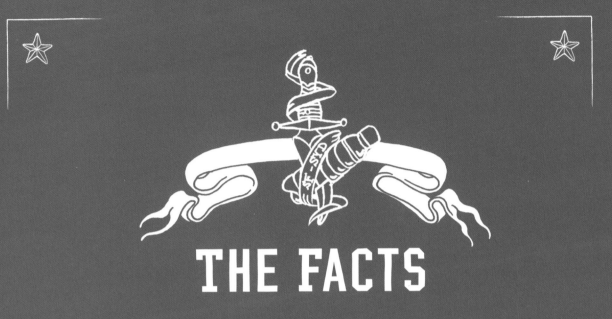

# THE FACTS

A DEAD TURTLE FOUND IN HAWAII HAD MORE THAN 1,000 BITS OF PLASTIC IN ITS STOMACH AND INTESTINES.

IN SWEDEN, 80 PERCENT OF PET PLASTIC BOTTLES ARE RECYCLED. IN THE U.S., ONLY 15 PERCENT ARE REUSED.

ENOUGH ENERGY TO POWER 750,000 HOMES FOR A YEAR IS SAVED BY RECYCLING PLASTIC CONTAINERS IN THE U.S.

CAPTAIN CHARLES MOORE (BOTTOM LEFT) HAS LED RESEARCH ON THE GREAT PACIFIC GARBAGE PATCH, SURVEYING HOW MUCH PLASTIC IS THERE AND HOW IT AFFECTS MARINE LIFE.

# NINETY SECONDS WITH CAPTAIN PLASTIC

Charles Moore is the accidental environmental crusader. A furniture restorer and amateur sailor, Moore was returning to Long Beach, California, from Honolulu at the conclusion of the Transpacific Yacht Race in 1997 when he took a long shortcut through a windless area that sailboats typically avoid. What he found there shocked him: floating shampoo bottles, fishing nets, and other plastic debris as far as he could see for day upon day. He since has launched the Algalita Marine Research Foundation and uncovered the fact that it's the plastic you don't see that is the real problem.

### WHY NOT JUST CLEAN UP THE GARBAGE PATCH?

For starters, it covers an enormous area, and the amount of debris entering the gyre every day is huge. A nonprofit group called Project Kaisei is studying the feasibility of trawling the gyre. This Herculean effort might collect 100 tons of plastic in a month. In that same time period, 30 tons of plastic waste will enter the Pacific from Los Angeles rivers alone. Add in the flow from the Mekong, Yangtze, and Yellow rivers, as well as Tokyo and discharge from ships, and easily ten to one hundred times as much plastic will enter the gyre as Kaisei takes out. We have to stop the flow.

### HOW SERIOUS IS THE PROBLEM OF PLASTIC MARINE DEBRIS?

Our plastic footprint is taking a greater toll than our carbon footprint, and we're just beginning to understand it. At the bottom of the food chain is the tiny lantern fish (*Myctophidae*), which makes up 50 percent of fish biomass. They are the food for all of the other fish in the ocean. We sampled 671 of these 2-inch-long fish and found that 35 percent had plastic particles in their stomachs. One fish had 84 pieces of plastic. Lantern fish hide a mile down in the ocean during the day and feed in the surface layer at night. With plastic inside them, they have to fight this flotation to go back down a mile deep during the day. If lantern fish fail, we risk losing all the other fish in the ocean.

### HOW'D WE GET INTO THIS JAM?

People are addicted to the throwaway lifestyle. We have a wasteful economy that thrives on obsolescence and rapid turnover. The majority of waste is packaging, or what I call fast-track trash. It's just grating to see packaging that is hundreds of times the volume and weight of the product inside it.

### WHAT'S THE SOLUTION?

Right off, we need controls in our storm-water systems, paid for by industry, to capture plastic run-off. We also need extended producer responsibility. Companies need to create an infrastructure to take back their products at the end of their useful lives and their packaging. The burden can't be on the taxpayer. There has to be a deposit on plastic bottles. Since plastic lasts forever, let's make stuff out of it that lasts forever. Throwaways should be degradable.

PLASTIC WASTE HAS TRAGIC CONSEQUENCES—
AS SEEN IN THIS PACIFIC SEABIRD, WHOSE
STOMACH WAS FULL OF BOTTLE CAPS AND
OTHER GARBAGE.

deep blue sea. That was the visible garbage many miles from the gyre. How many billions of plastic particles swirled in the waters around us?

. . .

Taken together, accumulation zones in our oceans cover 25 percent of the earth's surface. Think about that for a minute. We have unwittingly fouled one-quarter of our planet with plastic, much of it used for a few minutes and then chucked. Surely this is one of the most tragic manifestations of our consumer culture.

MOST VARIETIES OF PLASTIC FALL TO PIECES, BUT THEY NEVER DISAPPEAR. PLASTIC IS SIMPLY TOO NEW ON THE NATURAL SCENE FOR ANY ENZYME TO HAVE EVOLVED TO CRACK IT APART.

We are only beginning to understand the full dimensions of the problem with plastics in the ocean. University of Plymouth marine biologist Richard Thompson has identified an entire class of plastic particles too small for the untrained human eye to detect. These "microplastics," sized from 5 millimeters down to 20 microns wide (the period at the end of this sentence is about 30 times bigger), float in the water column, settle into sediments, and become part of the beach. Thompson's testing equipment couldn't detect even smaller pieces, but he's certain they are out there. So where are these minute plastic particles coming from? A big source is plastic used as abrasive blast media in industrial applications, like cleaning boat hulls, or as scrubbing microbeads in cosmetic products like body wash and skin exfoliant (talk about really dumb uses of plastic!). But by far the leading source is simply larger pieces of plastic deteriorating into tiny bits.

# PLASTICTROSS

Albatrosses will fly hundreds, sometimes thousands of miles in search of food for their chicks. They are on the hunt for squid , fish eggs and any other ocean delight that happens to be floating on the surface of the water, however tragically this now also means plastic!! So rather than returning home to serve up a healthy and nutritious meal for their young ones, the Chicks are forced to feast on bottle caps, lighters, fishing lures and many other single use plastics. **The Outcome?** The chicks starve to death, with stomachs full of plastic. Scientists estimate that around the world, up to one million seabirds and 100,000 marine mammals and sea turtles die each year from eating plastic. This can stop today!!

**REFUSE SINGLE USE PLASTICS!**

## PLASTIC BEACH

When sand is completely obscured by plastic garbage, does a beach cease being a beach and become something else entirely? A *pleach* perhaps? Until recently, South Point on the big island of Hawaii was among the trashiest beaches in the world. The point and adjoining Kamilo Beach thrust outward into the swirling Great Pacific Garbage Patch like a giant ladle, scooping out plastic flotsam. Fishing nets, flip-flops, cigarette lighters, sunglasses, bottle caps, straws, pens, soda bottles—every conceivable artifact of the plastic age—can pile up over a foot deep. The same scene is repeated at scores of other Hawaiian beaches and at thousands of others around the world.

The plastic tide began to turn at Kamilo Beach starting in 2003 with several major beach cleanups organized by the Hawaii Wildlife Fund. Volunteers carted off hundreds of sacks filled with waste, while forklifts pulled away massive tangles of marooned fishing net. Cleanups continue to this day; a recent one removed 5 tons of plastic trash. Today, Kamilo Beach is far cleaner than it once was, but it will never again be pristine—not as long as the garbage patch still exists.

Most varieties of plastic fall to pieces, but they never disappear. No organism can break them down into their raw building blocks. Lignin, the strengthening component in the cell walls of woody plants, is a polymer like plastic, and a more complex one at that, yet it biodegrades. Plastic is simply too new on the natural scene for any enzyme to have evolved to crack it apart.

However, new research shows that the action of sun and salt water does to several varieties of plastic—polystyrene, the plastic in Styrofoam; polycarbonate, the hard plastic in screwdriver handles; and epoxy resin,

### IN A COSMIC BOOMERANG, THE GARBAGE PATCH AND THE TOXIC RESIDUE FROM DECADES OF PESTICIDE RUNOFF AND INDUSTRIAL POLLUTION HAVE BECOME A PART OF US.

which is commonly used to protect ship hulls from rusting—what microorganisms can't. And the results are unsettling. Katsuhiko Saido at Japan's Nihon University discovered that in typical ocean conditions, these plastics degrade into endocrine-disrupting bisphenol A (BPA) in the cases of polycarbonate and epoxy resin, and into BPA and PS oligomer, another endocrine disrupter, as well as cancer-causing styrene monomer, dimer, and trimer, in the case of polystyrene. (Polystyrene bears a 6 in the recycling code, polycarbonate a 7.) When Saido and his team sampled sand and ocean water at two hundred sites in twenty countries, they found BPA at levels they considered "significant," from 0.01 parts per million to 50 ppm.

Set loose in the ocean, plastics like the PET in water bottles, HDPE in milk jugs, LDPE in grocery bags, and polypropylene in ketchup bottles will slowly photodegrade: The sun's photons snap the long polymer chains. In time, the plastic object will disintegrate into smaller and smaller pieces but never into simpler compounds. Wind, waves, and rain accelerate the process. At the stage where the plastic bits are about the size of a BB, they're called mermaid tears, surf pills, or nurdles. Hypothetically, the process of miniaturization will continue to the molecular level. So every bit of #1, #2, #3, #4, and #5 plastic ever produced, with the exception of the small amount incinerated, is still out there somewhere.

Smaller objects have more surface area relative to their mass than larger objects. We all learned that in geometry class. Now get ready for a little bit of organic chemistry and biology, because plastic acts to sponge up such toxic chemicals as dioxin, PCBs, DDE, and a host of herbicides and pesticides present in the ocean in dilute quantities. These are oily, or fat soluble, substances, and plastic loves oily stuff. It's a match made in hell. The smaller the piece of plastic, the more effective it is at swabbing up nasty chemicals, and the more likely it is to enter the food chain by being ingested by a filter-feeding animal. An examination of polypropylene resin nurdles in Tokyo Bay found their load of PCBs and DDE at levels 100,000 to 1,000,000 times higher than that of the surrounding seawater.

And here we get to the insidious danger—the "Why should I care?" wake-up call—posed by marine plastics. PCBs, BPA, and their ilk are bad actors because they are estrogen imitators. Yep, hard to believe, but thousands of man-made chemicals are mistaken for estrogen inside an animal host, including you and me. Plants like soybeans also create estrogen-imitating chemicals. Inside the body, these phony estrogens bind to receptors on the outer walls of cells in breast tissue, ovaries, testicles, and other sex organs reserved for real estrogen and androgen, the male sex hormone. Docked to a cell, these intruders can create havoc by blocking real sex hormones from doing their job and by turning on or hyping finely tuned natural processes usually dictated by the endocrine system.

Plastics *absorb* these devilish chemicals, but do they *adsorb*, or release, them when eaten? Until recently, the answer to that was uncertain. But investigations by Richard Thompson and colleagues at the University of Plymouth on sediment-swilling lugworms fed with contaminated microplastics, and by University of Tokyo toxicologist Hideshige Takada, who studied seabirds fed fish bearing PCB-laced plastic pellets, shows that persistent organic pollutants cross from the gut to the circulatory system.

These minuscule poison pills now threaten the entire food chain, including anyone who eats mussels, clams, oysters, lobsters, shrimp, and fish—that is, us! In a cosmic boomerang, the garbage patch and the toxic residue from decades of pesticide runoff and industrial pollution have become a part of us.

...

Plastic is not the enemy. With the *Plastiki* project and our development of Seretex, we're showing how to better understand plastic and use it in a smart way. We're working with our partners Hewlett-Packard (HP), Nike, and IWC to encourage them to find ways to use Seretex in their supply chains. HP is looking into using it in their laptop casings. With 15 million laptops sold last year, HP could exert huge influence on the market for recycled PET.

While we can and should use much less plastic, the fact is that plastic is a miraculous material with far more potential—and longer life span—than we give it credit for. A convincing case can be made that plastic's environmental benefits in terms of reducing overall fuel use through lighter-weight vehicles and in shipping lighter goods outweigh the negatives. If we're smarter about how we use it and dispose of it, we can stem the plastic tide.

# CREW PROFILE: MAX JOURDAN

Besides playing a wicked game of Perudo, mending torn sails, and being a wizard in the tiny and ill-equipped kitchen on *Plastiki,* Max is first and foremost an accomplished maker of documentaries. He was aboard *Plastiki* to film footage for a two-part series for the National Geographic Channel about the construction and voyage of the boat that airs in spring 2011. His films—*The Toughest Cop in America, Las Vegas Comes to China,* and *The Couple with 27 Children,* to name a few—have appeared on broadcast television in England, France, and the United States.

### WHERE IS HOME?
London. Gray and wet. I wish I could call California my home.

### AS A FILMMAKER, WHAT'S UNIQUE ABOUT SHOOTING AT SEA?
Everything gets very wet. And you need to get over the vomit-inducing action of looking through a small viewfinder when everything is rolling and pitching.

### FAVORITE PART OF THE DAY ON PLASTIKI?
When I wasn't filming and just chilling.

### LEAST FAVORITE ONBOARD DUTY?
Cleaning the toilet. I only cleaned it once and never used it.

### WHERE DID YOU LEARN TO COOK SO WELL?
When I was about fourteen, Mum said she wasn't going to cook another meal. (Don't ask why.) And she didn't. So I was stuck.

### WILL YOU EVER AGAIN TAKE FOR GRANTED A MOTIONLESS, QUIET BED?
I actually really enjoyed the nightly motion and cacophony.

### WORST CRAVING WHILE AT SEA?
Don't go there.

### WOULD YOU ENDORSE ONE MONTH AT SEA FOR EVERYONE?
Yes. Best thing for the body and soul.

### DID YOU EVER COME CLOSE TO FALLING OVERBOARD WITH YOUR "TACKLE OUT?"
Yes, I did. But I did everything in my power to avoid such an embarrassing situation.

### WAS REACHING AUSTRALIA EVER IN DOUBT IN YOUR MIND?
Yes, all the time.

### YOUR LASTING IMPRESSION OF THE PACIFIC?
Vast, blue and wild. And I miss it so.

THIS IS THE GARBAGE PATCH: MILES OF OCEAN
FOULED WITH TINY PLASTIC PELLETS, THE
REMAINS OF COUNTLESS LARGER PLASTIC ITEMS.

## AN S.O.S. ON WORLD OCEANS DAY:
## SAVE OUR SEAS; SAVE OURSELVES

### BY SYLVIA EARLE

Since I began exploring the ocean as a marine scientist fifty years ago, more has been learned about the ocean than during all preceding history. At the same time, more has been lost.

Two weeks ago I testified before the U.S. Congress on the ecological impact of the oil spill in the Gulf of Mexico. I did so with perspective gained while sloshing around oiled beaches and marshes among dead and dying animals, diving under sheets of oily water, and for years—as a founder and executive of engineering companies—working with those in the oil industry responsible for developing and operating sophisticated equipment in the sea.

As chief scientist of the National Oceanic and Atmospheric Administration from 1990 to 1992, I devoted much of my time to the aftermath of two major catastrophic oil spills: the accidental loss of 11 million gallons of crude oil

from the *Exxon Valdez* in Alaska and the deliberate release of 462 million gallons into the Persian Gulf as an act of "ecological terrorism" by Iraq.

As tragic as they were, nothing compares with last summer's oil spill that gushed from a mile below the surface of the Gulf of Mexico.

The near-freezing temperature and high pressure combined with a lack of suitable equipment to effectively deal with an operational failure at that depth magnified the damage being done to "America's Mediterranean," a trinational treasure, the planet's ninth-largest body of water, and, therefore, a globally significant part of Earth's life-support system.

As recipient of the 2009 TED Prize, I was given an opportunity to make one wish "large enough to change the world"—a wish that brought with it a commitment by the TED community to help make it come true.

My wish? To use all the means at our disposal—films, expeditions, the Web, new submarines, and more—to ignite public support for a global network of Marine Protected Areas—"hope spots" large enough to save and restore the ocean, the blue heart of the planet.

June 8 marks the official United Nations' World Oceans Day. In light of the recent Deepwater Horizon oil spill, never has there been a more critical time to reflect on the importance of the oceans to humanity and, more important, to work together to save the earth's blue heart.

It once seemed that, as with the ocean as a whole, the gulf was so big and so resilient that nothing we could do could harm it. The benefits, we believed, would always be there, no matter how large the trawls, how long the nets, how numerous the hooks for catching ocean wildlife, or how many, how long, or how deep the pipelines, drilling operations, seismic surveys, or production rigs.

But destructive fishing practices have sharply depleted ocean wildlife, some by 90 percent in fifty years, including sharks, tunas, marlin, menhaden, groupers, snappers, tarpon, turtles, shrimp, crabs, and others.

Half of the coral reefs are gone or are in a state of sharp decline. Dead zones in the sea, unknown until recent decades, are rapidly proliferating. Excess carbon dioxide is accelerating global warming, sea level rise, ocean acidification, and overall climate change. These are factors that impact the nature of the world from the highest mountain peak to the deepest ocean trench.

Life in the sea, after all, supports the basic processes that we all take for granted: the water cycle, the oxygen cycle, the carbon cycle, and much more. With every breath we take, every drop of water we drink, we are dependent on the existence of Earth's living ocean.

So what can we do to save the oceans, and, in doing so, save ourselves? In April 2010, as part of the TED Mission Blue Voyage in the Galápagos Islands, we launched the Mission Blue campaign, an effort to garner public support to call on governments to establish a global network of Marine Protected Areas.

Marine Protected Areas help recover marine environments in order to provide natural solutions to critical environmental challenges. They provide safe havens for ocean wildlife to recover and maintain healthy biodiversity, supporting habitats that act as carbon sinks, removing $CO_2$ from the air, and generating the majority of atmospheric oxygen.

Mission Blue, however, is only one part of the solution. Everyone has the power to make a difference. The trick is to use that power, whatever it is, to take positive actions.

In a recent Skype interview with David de Rothschild, we challenged the world to find their personal *Plastiki*, their personal Mission Blue.

What will be your solution? You can help save the oceans and, in so doing, save ourselves.

. . .

*Sylvia Earle is an oceanographer and the founder of Mission Blue.*

# 5
## CLEAR SAILING

SAILING DEEP INTO THE PACIFIC HOLDS
MANY SURPRISES: LOTS OF HEAT
AND NOISE, VERY LITTLE SEA LIFE AND—
ON EARTH DAY—A BABY!

ENTERING OUR FIFTH WEEK OF SAILING THE PACIFIC
OCEAN, APPROXIMATE POSITION 1,000 MILES SOUTHEAST OF
HAWAII, IT BECAME APPARENT THAT WHOEVER NAMED OUR PLANET
IS GUILTY OF A TERRIBLE OVERSIGHT. "EARTH" SHOULD
JUST AS WELL BE KNOWN AS "OCEAN."

After all, saltwater covers 72 percent of our planet's surface. The Pacific Ocean alone—whose midpoint *Plastiki* hadn't yet reached—is larger than the land mass all of the continents and subcontinents and innumerable islands combined. Ours is, indeed, a blue planet.

Water was much on my mind. It preoccupied my waking and sleeping thoughts. It was everywhere, and it was nowhere. I floated on a 14,000-foot-deep layer of it. I viewed 360 degrees of endless aquatic horizon, day in, day out. I slowly marinated in its salty residue, which had invaded my every pore. There was all of that, yes, but, more to the point, I was parched and really, really wanted to go for a swim but wasn't allowed.

As we progressed toward a first stop in the Line Islands, our streak of rainless days grew, and our supply of water shrank. We were dogged by a high-pressure zone that had parked in the eastern Pacific. Weather systems usually move through from west to east at a good clip, but the weather across the northern hemisphere was out of whack that spring due to an unusually strong El Niño. To avoid the nearly calm winds at the center of

this large fair-weather system, we altered *Plastiki*'s route to sail more directly south from San Francisco before swinging west. The big high sagged south and west with us, almost as though in pursuit. To quibble over the gift of steady seas and sunny days would seem to invite Neptune's revenge, but we needed rain.

As we sailed south across the 10th parallel, the air and water temperatures rose to tropical levels. Away went the rain gear and fleece (not to be seen again until we encountered Australia's winter winds), out came T-shirts and shorts. Beneath the tropical sun, our translucent plastic dome home became ghastly hot. The simple act of making a pot of tea or preparing dinner on the stove would drive the indoor temperature to a sauna setting.

With daytime temperatures climbing well into the 90s and the wind slackening, getting through the heat of the day became a game of ducking out of the sun and staying as still as possible. At 11:00, I could hide out in the shade cast by the mizzen. At 2:00, the shadow from the mainsail offered relief. At 3:00, I knew I could

WITH THE ROUGH SEAS OF *PLASTIKI*'S FIRST WEEKS
BEHIND THEM, THE CREW FOUND THEMSELVES
WITH PLENTY OF TIME AS THEIR SHIP MOVED
SLOWLY TOWARD THE LINE ISLANDS.

cower in the small triangle of shade by the cabin door. Olav, bless his Norwegian heart, was largely unfazed by the heat. In fact, he sought the sun. "I love the heat and the sun. It gives me the necessary vitamins and the extra energy," he explained. He pranced around the deck in his boxers or less. He wouldn't let anyone miss his burlesque. "Hey, lewk, I'm naked," he'd yell while waggling his privates. Okay, Olav.

Midday was hardest to bear. Under the relentless sun, we sweltered. The urge to jump into the ocean was unbearable. However, swimming, we were told by Jo, was out of the question. The risk of a mishap and being left behind was too great. As long as the sails were up and the wind blowing, we weren't stopping. It might seem easy enough to keep up with a boat lumbering along at 2 knots, about the cruising speed of a geriatric's electric scooter, but *Plastiki* would outpace even a strong swimmer. Getting back on board presented its own set of difficulties. The boat deck rides high above the waterline, and the soda bottles and their racking systems didn't offer much to grab hold of. A swimmer's arm strength might give out before he could clamber back on deck. So we filled the long watch hours hatching plans to get wet.

"I will pretend I have fallen overboard, and, David, you come to my rescue," suggested Olav. "Jo will have to stop the boat then."

"We'd still have to grab the man-overboard rope off

HOTTING UP AS WE FLOW SOUTH 2 THE EQUATOR, GETTING A LITTLE MORE TOASTY INSIDE THE CABIN. I'M OBSESSED BY FLYING FISH! 2 FLY AND SWIM = MAGIC
@DREXPLORE 12:18 A.M., APRIL 13, 2010

PLASTIKI'S FIRST SWIM WAS A WELCOME BREAK FROM THE HEAT OF THE TROPICS—AND THE FIRST CHANCE TO CHECK UP ON THE HULLS. ALL BOTTLES WERE ACCOUNTED FOR.

the back of the boat and hang on. That'll cause a lot of chafing and rope burn," I reminded him.

"What about using the seat harness Mr. T uses to climb the mainmast to rig a dunking seat off of the boom?" I countered.

"No, Mr. T's too protective of his harness," said Vern.

"Or we could take some of the spare netting, rig it with diving weights, and tie it off the back," I suggested. "Then you'd jump off the bow, swim between the hulls, and get caught in the net."

"But how would you get out of the net and back on the boat?" wondered Olav.

"How about blowing up that inflatable mattress, tying a rope around it for a handle, then lashing it to the net?" said Vern.

These brainstorming sessions could go on for hours. We considered the viability of every swimming option in excruciating detail. Admittedly, we were obsessed.

Weeks before, we had gone for our first and only swim. Brief though it was, that baptism in the Pacific was in my mind the highlight of the trip to date. On that particular day, the wind had died and the ocean lay perfectly still. Sky and water merged in intersecting planes of gray. The incessant din of water swirling and vibrating against plastic bottles—the soundtrack of the *Plastiki* voyage—had mercifully stopped. No sooner did Jo and Mr. T have the sails down than Olav had wriggled out of his clothes and dived into the ocean. His whoops and squeals got everyone's attention. Within seconds we had all jumped in, kicking, flipping, and laughing.

"Is anyone on the boat? Jo?" shouted Max.

"No, I'm right here," cried Jo.

Floating in the cool, incalculably deep, and sublimely blue Pacific, the nearest land a thousand miles away, I felt as free as I could ever hope to be.

### CREW VIEW: MAX JOURDAN

Turn ON, press RECORD, frame, focus, reframe. Welcome to my little rectangular world. Jo's liquid blue eyes crystallize on the LCD screen. Beautiful against the gray skies. Raw skin and bleached hair floating in the light breeze. I can sense the thoughts formulating on her lips. A small nudge: "What's up, Jo?"

"We're over a thousand miles from any landfall." Jo looks profoundly happy.

I think: "A thousand miles from nowhere is where the pilot lands his stricken plane and meets the Little Prince."

"What does that mean, Jo?"

"It means it would take someone quite a while to rescue us. It means we're alone."

The announcement is electric. It means we've got to be completely autonomous. Out here we can make up the rules. There's no law. No consumer society. We don't need to buy anything today. We're free now.

GIANT CARGO SHIPS WERE SOME OF THE ONLY
LIFE *PLASTIKI* ENCOUNTERED AT SEA.

"Jo, you star," I mutter, and pan across to a vision of freedom—watery, gray, with a cloud base so low you could reach out and touch it.

..........................

The increasingly serious situation with our water supply claimed a first victim on April 10. Watching the slow, silent death was difficult, especially for Jo. I refer to the demise of the rotating cylinder garden, which provided us with chard, kale, spinach, bok choy, and other leafy greens during the early weeks of the trip. Jo had arranged for Inka Biospheric Systems to design and install the clever hydroponic garden on the mizzenmast. Behind a shield of clear srPET grew ninety-six plants in a ridiculously small space. Specially arrayed vents kept the cylinder from overheating, and the top was designed to harvest rainwater. If, that is, it bothered to rain.

A hydroponic garden subjected to the equatorial sun is a thirsty beast. No one on board disagreed that this microfarm conveyed an important message about the potential for growing food in cramped shantytowns or desert areas, but a stark choice presented itself: Either the garden got water or we did. Fresh produce at sea is an amazing thing, something we looked forward to at dinner time. So we did our best to save the garden, from cloaking it against the harsh sun, to feeding it water mixed with urine, and finally removing half of the plants. It still guzzled water.

Jo was gallant in defense of her beloved veggies, but in the end the group spoke. We decided to pull the plug. Our consolation lay in the prospect of reviving the garden with tropical plants on arrival in the Line Islands.

Getting to the Line Islands wasn't much in doubt. The chain of eleven low atolls stretches across nearly

DAVID AND JO LAUNCHED A SATELLITE-TRACKED "MESSAGE IN THE BOTTLE" PREPARED BY ARTIST JAY LITTLE. CHECK ON ITS PROGRESS VIA PLASTIKI.COM.

"IT IS WHAT IT IS" BECAME MY MANTRA. THE "ARE WE THERE YET?" APPROACH WOULD HAVE ME CHECKING THE COMPUTERIZED NAVIGATION SYSTEM EVERY HOUR AND SLOWLY BEING DRIVEN MAD.

1,500 miles in a generally north-south alignment. Landing on one? That might be tricky. Our original intent was to resupply on Fanning Island, until we learned the island is in the throes of a severe drought and water was in short supply. Christmas Island became our backup destination. The largest and most populated of the Line Islands, Christmas Island has an international airport, the better for sending Vern, Max, and Olav on their way and welcoming their replacements, filmmaker Singeli Agnew, photographer Luca Babini, and environmentalist and good friend Graham Hill.

Navigating *Plastiki* toward a pinprick of solid ground in the middle of the Pacific would challenge Jo and Mr. T. "With a wind angle of between 120 and 150 degrees from the bow of the boat—ideal wind direction—we create about 15 degrees of leeway," said Jo. In other words, *Plastiki* moves like a crab. Three steps forward, one step sideways. Imagine tossing a Frisbee into the wind around a tree and landing it on a dime, and you'll have some sense of what our skippers were attempting. Knowing back in 2009 what we know now, we would have fine-tuned the boat's design to enhance steering and reduce sideways travel by lengthening the keel, installing dagger boards, and rigging a single central forestay rather than two off-center forestays. Next time, I guess.

Adding to the degree of difficulty in navigation, Jo and Mr. T had to factor in the shifting intertropical convergence zone, ITCZ, aka the Doldrums. This area of weak or nonexistent winds oscillates across the equator, usually between 5 degrees north and 5 degrees south. "At the moment, the ITCZ is breathing north over the Line Islands, then relaxing back toward the equator," explained Jo. "When the ITCZ is north, there will be no wind on our approach to the Line Islands. If we get trapped in the ITCZ, we could be stalled for a few days."

Vern was not cheered by this news. His impatience and anxiety, very understandably, escalated as April 23 drew closer. Max, who would also leave us at Christmas Island, prowled the deck like a man with a bad case of cabin fever. He was eager to reunite with his wife and young daughters back in France. Olav would be leaving us, too, but he wasn't in the least perturbed. Ambling across the Pacific is nothing new to him. He was part of the 2006 voyage of the *Tangaroa*, which averaged 2.4 knots in re-creating the *Kon-Tiki* expedition.

My attitude was the opposite of Vern and Max's. Setting foot on land, for me, was inconsequential. Sure, a freshwater shower and clean clothes would be welcome, but whether we got there in a week or three weeks really didn't matter. I had reached a state of adventure Zen, where I didn't know what day of the week it was. "It is what it is" became my mantra. Every day, every step of the journey I broke down into little victories. Daily routines of waking up, eating meals, tidying up, checking e-mail, and doing watch duty were my focus. With

WOW, THOUGHT IT WAS A SEABOUND UFO, BUT NO A 190 METER CARGO SHIP PASSED LESS THAN .5M FROM US IN THE DARK NIGHT

@JO_ROYLE 10:07 A.M., APRIL 10, 2010

*PLASTIKI*'S CREW ALWAYS GATHERED FOR DINNER, PREPARED BY THE DAY'S "MUM"—PREFERABLY MAX. GAMES OF PERUDO OFTEN FINISHED THE DAY.

months more to go, this is where I needed to be in my head. The "Are we there yet?" approach would have me checking the computerized navigation system every hour and slowly being driven mad.

With roughly one week remaining before we touched land and half of the team disappeared, I was regretting not getting to know Olav better. He is an extraordinary character and one of the most unintentionally hilarious people I've met. How, you might reasonably ask, is it possible to spend a month with someone in a living-room-size space and not know every intimate detail of his or her life? It turns out Olav and I had lived parallel and infrequently intersecting existences since leaving San Francisco. By virtue of our watch system, we were a crew divided. We had the Jo Team of Olav and Max, and the Mr. T Team of Vern and me. Perhaps it's only human nature, but the team setup

gradually led to some silly tribalism. Bickering cropped up over unequal water consumption, who snuck the last lemon custard or strawberry jam, and which team was shirking cleanup duties.

Despite our petty differences and diverging schedules, we came together every evening over dinner. We put the steering of the boat in the capable hands of Ash, our wind vane autopilot, and gathered to eat, whether inside squeezed around the galley table on those chilly, storm-tossed evenings or sprawled on the nubby plastic deck surface when the weather allowed. What the person whose night it was to play "Mum" might prepare was a surprise, usually pleasant, as with the healthy rice and vegetable dishes Jo concocted; but sometimes not, as when Olav served a gruel of overcooked mashed pasta. Max, however, was everyone's favorite Mum. A typical Max meal would feature homemade pita fresh from

the oven, black sesame–crusted mahi-mahi fillets, and braised kale and garlic served over brown rice. When Max cooked, cleanup was a breeze. Every bowl was scraped clean.

HEAVY, DARK CLOUDS FILLED THE SKY, AND A CURTAIN OF RAIN WAS FAST APPROACHING FROM THE SOUTHWEST. SHOWER TIME!

After dinner came game time, and the game of choice on *Plastiki* was Perudo. An ancient Peruvian dice game similar to liar's dice, Perudo rewards bluffing and guesswork, skills that our Frenchman, Max, came by naturally. He fancied himself a bit of a Perudo master.

"Crazy calls and preposterous gambles often pay off as a way of frightening the opponents and pulling wool over their eyes," is how he described his strategy. He had all his opponents sized up: "David de R., good bluffer; snake in the grass. Vern, a soft touch; the all-American boy takes the scheming, cheating, conniving Brits at face value. Olav, too distracted; his mind wanders at the sight of a beautiful cloud or lascivious thought. Dave T, plays with sunglasses on so difficult to tell his game, though usually breaks under pressure. Jo, plays it cool and lady-like; her game is quiet but determined, and she often has the advantage over the boisterous male crew."

### CREW VIEW: VERN MOEN

In the end, [*Plastiki*] is a community like anybody else's, albeit one compressed and culturally accelerated.

# CREW PROFILE: OLAV HEYERDAHL

In the field of adventure, the name Heyerdahl is royalty. Thor Heyerdahl's *Kon-Tiki* blew apart the prevailing "because it's there" notion of expeditions, introducing instead adventuring with a purpose. He also inspired generations of would-be explorers. A carpenter by trade and engineer by training, Olav had no intention of following in his famous grandfather's footsteps. That changed in 2005, when he received an invitation to join the *Tangaroa*, an expedition to replicate Thor Heyerdahl's epic *Kon-Tiki* voyage in every detail, only this time to get it right. Thor's own research after *Kon-Tiki* revealed that ancient mariners sailed faster, more-maneuverable rafts than his with the aid of multiple square-rigged sails and a system of centerboards. Olav signed on, and the crown was passed.

### WHAT'S IT LIKE GROWING UP HEYERDAHL?

In South America and the United States, the name really attracts attention. For me, it has always been a special feeling having such a famous man as a grandfather. I remember visiting him in Italy and Peru, hearing all of the stories, and being invited to the castle to have dinner with the king of Norway. That is special for a young man.

### WHAT MADE YOU JOIN THE TANGAROA EXPEDITION?

I was writing my final thesis in South Africa for civil engineering, and Torgeir Higraff, who was a journalist and amateur archaeologist, sent me an e-mail explaining how my grandfather was his childhood hero. We had the opportunity to build the kind of raft my grandfather would have built today.

### HOW DID TANGAROA DIFFER FROM KON-TIKI?

We steered with keels and a system of retractable centerboards. We went to the same atoll, Raroia, but we were able to take more of a western course.

With a sail area almost three times bigger than *Kon-Tiki*'s, we did it in 70 days. *Kon-Tiki* took 101. Also, when we got to Raroia, we made a safe landing.

### WHAT AMAZED YOU ABOUT YOUR GRANDFATHER'S EXPEDITION?

He was afraid of water when he sailed *Kon-Tiki*. He almost drowned in his youth.

### WHY PLASTIKI?

I have a famous last name, so to bring my name to a project or expedition, it has to be serious, no bull. My hopes for *Plastiki* are that people will become aware that we are misusing our planet. There will only be leftovers for generations to come. I hope this unique adventure will inspire others to get creative.

### WHAT MAKES FOR A SUCCESSFUL EXPEDITION?

You have to work together. You have to be friends. You can't let snoring or slurping food—small details—become irritating. Think big, adjust, and work together.

Households are bunks. There are two grocery stores, one in each hull. There's a library, a bar, a farm, a restaurant ("Max's"), and most of the other conveniences that we land crabs require. What makes this community exceptional, and what makes my trip on board *Plastiki* a special opportunity, is not only the way in which it has micro-mirrored our civilized world, but, better yet, that we are off the grid, sustainable, recyclable, and self-sufficient in, perhaps, the least accommodating environment in the world—making me reflect on why this is not possible on land.

........................

One of the quirks of *Plastiki*'s design is that the acoustics inside the cabin exaggerate what is actually going on outside. Seated at the tiller, you might hardly notice the mainmast and boom banging around. In the cabin, though, it would seem like you're sitting inside a bass drum while Led Zeppelin's John Bonham solos on "Moby Dick." On the late morning of April 24, Vern and I were asleep in the cabin when a tremendous commotion arose. Shouts rang out and feet pounded quickly across the deck. Either the boat was sinking or someone had fallen overboard.

"You think it's fine?" Vern asked. "They would have called us if it wasn't, right?"

"Ahh, damn, might as well see what's going on," I grumbled groggily.

Emerging from the cabin, Vern and I took in a bizarre scene. Everybody was naked or in some stage of disrobing and dashing to position themselves at strategic spots on deck, shampoo and soap in hand. One look overhead told me all I needed to know. Heavy, dark clouds filled the sky, and a curtain of rain was fast approaching from the southwest. Shower time!

On an ocean sailing adventure, salt is a force to be reckoned with. It fades and corrodes every material it comes in contact with. On skin, its effects are equally caustic. Salt cracks the skin at the fingertips and causes sores in sensitive areas like the groin, armpits, back of the legs, and between the toes and fingers. Jo and Mr. T repeatedly warned us of the dangers of "baboon butt," a rot that afflicts sailors who sit too long in damp shorts. The resulting sores become so painful that sitting down is practically impossible. To find relief, sailors have been known to dangle their bare asses off the side of a boat or back their tender butt cheeks up against a cool aluminum mast.

With limited fresh water on board and nothing falling from the sky, our only resource for getting clean had been a saltwater shower using a bucket and our sponsor Kiehl's 3-in-1 body wash and shampoo formulated for saltwater. While good for getting rid of grime and sweat, these cold dousings still left us covered with sticky salt. That's where a few rubs in the right places with a baby wipe came into play. For feeling truly clean, nothing compares to a rainwater bath. In our first weeks at sea, some promising-looking clouds sent everyone scurrying. Where's my towel? Where's my soap? The prime spot to be was near the base of the mast, where you could count on a torrent of rainwater rushing down the sail. On those couple of occasions, we were sudsed up, but the clouds spat rain for only a few minutes. "Oh, hang on. Hang on. What? What? Oh, shit." You never saw such disappointment on the faces of six foamed humans.

This time, however, it rained good and proper. A regular tropical downpour. Some of us danced deliriously. I lay down and let the rain pelt me. I washed my hair, got the salt out of every nook and crevice, and even soaped and rinsed the clothes I'd been wearing. It felt amazing to be clean, really clean, for the first time in thirty-three days. We filled up three large jerry cans full of rainwater and chugged glass after glass of the sweetest water any of us had ever tasted.

• • •

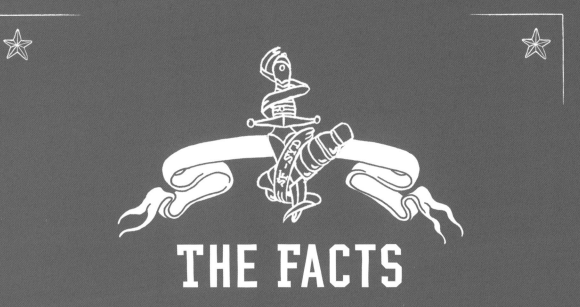

# THE FACTS

POPULATIONS OF LARGE FISH SUCH AS TUNA, COD,
SWORDFISH, AND MARLIN, HAVE DECLINED
BY AS MUCH AS NINETY PERCENT.

SIXTY-THREE PERCENT OF WORLDWIDE FISH STOCKS
ARE EXPLOITED AND NEED REBUILDING.

PEOPLE EAT AN AVERAGE OF 36 POUNDS OF FISH
AND OTHER SEAFOOD EACH YEAR.

ONE EVER-PRESENT WONDER OF THE VOYAGE
WAS THE PACIFIC ITSELF, WHICH RANGED FROM
STILL AND BLUE TO RAGING AND GRAY.

## BEST PIRATE JOKES EVER

The crew of the *Plastiki* has a thing for pirates. Okay, it's David who really has a thing for "pyrats." Must be all the swashbuckling, marauding, and wearing of outrageous hats. When the crew put out a request for pirate jokes to its Facebook friends, they didn't disappoint:

WHAT'S A PIRATE'S FAVORITE FOOD? ARRRRRTICHOKES. FAVORITE DECORATOR? MAAAARRRRRTHA STEWART. FAVORITE CLOTHING PATTERN? ARRRRRGGGYLLE.
—ALAN CURRY GAMBLE

WHAT DO YOU CALL A PIRATE WITH TWO EYES AND TWO LEGS? ANSWER: ROOKIE! —MAYA SOBININA

A PIRATE WALKS INTO A BAR. BARTENDER NOTICES HE HAS A SHIP'S WHEEL STICKING OUT OF THE FLY OF HIS TROUSERS. BARTENDER ASKS, "WHAT'S UP WITH THAT?" PIRATE RESPONDS, "ARRRR! IT'S DRIVIN' ME NUTS!!"
—RALPH MANGLASS

LITTLE JOHNNY GOES TO SCHOOL ON COSTUME DAY DRESSED LIKE A PIRATE. TEACHER SAYS, "GREAT COSTUME, JOHNNY. WHERE'S YOUR BUCCANEERS?" AND JOHNNY SAYS, "UNDER MY BUCCAN' HAT." —EDWARD WALKER

Q: WHAT DOES A PEG-LEG PIRATE DO WHEN HE'S DONE WITH THE HIGH SEAS?
A: WORK AT IHOP. —JAHNYS MOODY

NOT A PIRATE JOKE, BUT A PLASTIC ONE: THIS CRAZY GUY WALKS INTO AN INSANE ASYLUM WEARING NOTHING BUT PLASTIC WRAP AS SHORTS. THE DOCTOR WALKS IN AND TELLS HIM, "I CAN CLEARLY SEE YOUR NUTS!" —HEIDI SIMPSON

## CREW VIEW: JO ROYLE

Being at sea is so peaceful on your mind, as you spend each day simply responding to the needs of the boat and what the weather throws at you. You eliminate all the land noise, the continuous distractions, no decisions on what to wear, how to make the most out of the hours you have, whether to do this or that. On the other hand, the boat never stops moving, the noise of the water rushing through the bottles never stops, nor the sound of approaching waves, the wind whistling in the rig, vibrations and creaking of the rig as we ride over the waves, the music of the wind generators charging. The movement never stops either; even now as I type I am bracing my body against each wave. We often walk around the place looking like toddlers taking their first steps.

........................

In the wee hours of Earth Day, April 22, while *Plastiki* was still hundreds of miles from making landfall, William Grizzly Moen decided to make his debut early. Vern received the phone call he'd been both anticipating and dreading: His wife Melinda's water had broken, and she was in labor. There was no way now that he'd witness the birth in person. He'd have to phone it in. By daybreak, Melinda was in the advanced stages of labor, and Vern was crouched at the computer desk with the satellite phone clutched to his ear. "There's a head? There's the head!" he shouted. He gave us blow-by-blow descriptions of the action occurring in a hospital delivery room nearly 4,000 miles away. "This is the mother of all ironies," he said, turning to Olav and me. "I'm out here trying to save the earth, and my wife is giving birth on Earth Day."

At that moment, I received an urgent e-mail from Adventure Ecology's communications director in London, Katie Tilleke, reminding me that I had a live telephone interview scheduled right away with Al Jazeera television network for an Earth Day special about plastics in the oceans. Charles Moore of the Algalita Marine Research Foundation was the other guest. I told Katie there was no way I would make Vern get off the phone. The interview would have to take place on a Skype video call. As Katie scrambled to make the switch, we received word that a friend of Vern and Melinda's had circumvented the hospital's rules and arranged for Vern to watch the delivery on Skype.

As I talked to the producer at Al Jazeera, who informed me we were going live in three minutes, Vern

> FELL ASLEEP ON THE FORE DECK UNDER AN AWNING, WOKEN UP TO THE SUN TRYING TO TRACK ME DOWN, THE BODY'S HYDRATION LEVEL IS MIDDLE OF THE RD!
> @DREXPLORE 3:07 P.M., APRIL 14, 2010

shouted, "There's a head coming out of her vagina!" He was crying and emotional and getting more and more excited. As I went live with the television correspondent, Jo was in front of me trying to add Vern's friend's number into the Skype program, Max was filming, Olav was watching most amusedly, my Skype flashed as Vern's wife tried to connect, and Vern was shouting, "My wife is having a baby! I need to get on to Skype!" All of this is taking place in a space no bigger than a toolshed. "Mr. Rothschild, talk us through the plastic issue...," the Al Jazeera newscaster was saying. I made a stab at trying to concentrate, but finally I just said, "Look, one of our crew members is having a baby. I have to go." Click. I can only imagine what Charles Moore and the correspondent were thinking as the line went dead.

## INSIDE A WHALE'S STOMACH

Did junk food kill a 36-foot gray whale that washed up dead on a beach near Seattle in May 2010? Biologists aren't sure whether the whale mistook garbage for food or accidentally swept it in during normal feeding, but when they cut open its stomach, here's what they found:

5 lengths of fabric

2 lengths of duct tape

1 sock

3 feet of electrical tape

1 sweatpant leg

1 golf ball

2 towels

fishing line

15 inches of green rope

1 Capri-Sun juice packet

3 feet of nylon rope

1 red plastic cylinder

2 grocery bags

30 scraps of plastic bags

EARTH DAY WAS A HIGH POINT OF THE VOYAGE:
INTERVIEWS HELPED BEAM *PLASTIKI*'S MESSAGE
OUT TO THE WORLD, AND VERN WOULD SOON
WELCOME HIS FIRST CHILD.

At 10:18 A.M., Melinda gave one last push. "It's a boy! Whoo, whoo, it's a boy! I love you!" yelled Vern. "He's going to forgive his father for not being there. He's going to understand the adventure." Hugs and heartfelt congratulations filled the tiny cabin. We were happy to confirm via video that little William definitely did not have a handlebar mustache like his dad. "That was difficult. To see my wife going through all that and not being able to touch her," reflected Vern. "It felt like watching a professional basketball player—you just watch, captivated, in awe, at how that person is able to do that. Melinda was so strong and confident that I was almost lost for words and emotion. She just knew what she needed to do and did it."

If time seemed to slow to a crawl after the excitement of witnessing the delivery of Vern's mid-Pacific, Earth Day baby, it was probably because *Plastiki* was barely making 1 knot. At 3 degrees north of the equator, the wind all but died. We were making forward progress, but on a trajectory that would have us miss Christmas Island by nearly 100 miles. Next stop, Samoa.

Jo, Mr. T, and I wanted to land *Plastiki* under her own power, but that wasn't going to happen. *Plastiki* had

TODAY WE HAD A MEETING REGARDING WHETHER OR NOT WE WOULD MOVE OUR CLOCKS BACK AN HOUR. THE MEETING LASTED AN HOUR. SERIOUSLY.
@VERN_MOEN 8:30 A.M., APRIL 15, 2010

a mind of her own. Were it not for our commitments to Max, Olav, and Vern, I would have been happy to let the wind take us to the next island, whatever that might be.

TRAPPED ON THE SLOWER-THAN-PLANNED *PLASTIKI*, VERN USED SKYPE TO WITNESS THE BIRTH OF WILLIAM MOEN, FITTINGLY ON EARTH DAY.

SLEEPING WHILE TRAVELING AT 6 KNOTS ON THE PLASTIKI IS LIKE FALLING ASLEEP ON THE SIDE OF A FREEWAY THAT'S FULL OF SPEEDING SEMITRUCKS DRAGGING BROKEN RADIATORS BEHIND THEM.

@VERN_MOEN 12:42 P.M., APRIL 18, 2010

We had the food, and now we had the necessary water. We were in constant contact with expedition manager Matthew Grey, who had been on the ground on Christmas Island for several weeks making preparations for our arrival. "Uh, Matt, we're going to need a tow to get in," radioed Jo. "Got it. Already have one lined up," replied Matt.

Hours later, a plume of black smoke appeared on the horizon. As it drew closer, the source was revealed to be the most god-awful-looking rust bucket. Sun-bleached tarps draped every square foot of deck. Massive lifeboats dangled precariously from either side. It looked perfect for drug smuggling.

"Matt, is that you? What's going on?" I radioed.

"I've got your rescue," he replied. "This is the *Moa Moa*, the ferry that runs between Christmas and Fanning islands. We're going to pick you up."

## PLASTIC SURGERY: HOPE ON A ROPE

A funny thing happened on the way to the landfill: Plastic water and soda bottles in southern Brazil came back to life as high-performance rope. Each month, 700 tons of empties arrive at Arteplas's production facility and exit as colorful, woven, 100-percent-recycled rope prized by ranchers, sailors, and rock climbers. The company has added four hundred jobs to the local economy, and its ropes use 70 percent less energy than ropes made of virgin plastic. Arteplas rope is available for sale at canadianoutdoorequipment.com.

Matt had persuaded the captain that it was worth his while to take a sizable detour from his usual return route to Fanning Island. (About those rumors of cash changing hands, I have no comment.) The only thing is, the captain neglected to inform his one hundred or so passengers of the change in itinerary. As the *Moa Moa* maneuvered into position for a tow, we could see scores of passengers on the deck. Several were strumming guitars, some were waving, and more than a few looked confused as to why they were hooking up to this strange-looking plastic boat and not steaming toward home.

The tow to Christmas Island wasn't the proudest moment in our long voyage, nor was it the most pleasing. For twelve hours we bobbed up and down in the wake of the *Moa Moa* as she chugged along. We were caught in the ferry's slipstream of diesel fumes and biting flies. After thirty-nine days traversing a pure, watery wilderness, civilization never looked so unfamiliar.

DAVID DE ROTHSCHILD RAISES ONE
OF *PLASTIKI*'S SAILS.

# THE STARK REALITY OF A
# THROWAWAY SOCIETY

## BY IAN KIERNAN

I grew up on the shores of Sydney Harbor, and I fondly remember exploring the crystal-clear pools, observing the unique and bountiful marine life. Shells and driftwood, cuttlefish bones and dried seaweed littered the sand. That was the only debris from the ocean beyond that I saw.

Fast-forward a few decades, and there I was again, on the shores of Sydney Harbor cleaning up a very different kind of litter. It was 1989, and I was leading the first ever Clean Up Day on Sydney Harbor, and 40,000 other Sydneysiders were removing hundreds of tons of accumulated plastic, polystyrene, aluminum cans, glass bottles, dumped cars, and shopping trolleys.

This event led to Clean Up Australia, which then became the global Clean Up the World movement involving organizations and communities in 130 countries.

The dramatic change in my life was due to rubbish. What I saw while sailing solo around the world in the late 1980s changed me forever. Instead of the stark beauty of the deep blue oceans, I sailed through mile after mile of debris.

Plastic of all types, discarded fishing nets, and polystyrene buoys blanketed the surface of the ocean. This scene was repeated in all of the oceans I crossed, and the remnants of an increasingly throwaway society greeted me at each port.

I resolved then and there to make a difference, to take action to raise awareness about the damage our wasteful habits were having on our oceans. The rubbish in our oceans is not only ugly—it kills.

Turtles with the rings of plastic bottles around their necks, choking to death. Dolphins caught in old fishing nets, drowning because they can't break free. And seabirds drowning because of the fishing line wrapped around their wings. Between 700,000 and 1 million seabirds are killed each year by marine debris such as discarded fishing line and plastic bags.

There are two main sources of marine debris. There is the rubbish that comes from the land and the wind-blown rubbish that people leave behind. There is also ocean-based debris, and this is just as nasty. It includes fishing lines and nets; offshore oil and gas rig/platform debris; waste from merchant ships; and garbage from recreational and tourist vessels.

Every day, ships jettison 5.5 million pieces of rubbish into the sea. But it's not just ships that are trashing our oceans. We are all part of the problem. An estimated 7 million tons of rubbish arrives in the world's oceans each and every year.

Most of this rubbish is plastic. This is not surprising, because plastic never actually goes away; it simply breaks up into smaller and smaller pieces. Plastic makes up about 80 percent of all marine debris—plastic shopping bags alone make up 10 percent. And when that plastic breaks down into tiny little pieces, it is often swallowed by marine creatures and enters the food chain.

If all that floating plastic rubbish isn't eaten by marine life, it eventually washes ashore. To get your mind around just how much marine rubbish washes up on our shores, consider this: A Marine Debris Survey at Cape Arnhem in northern Australia counted, identified, and collected all the rubbish that washed up on a 5-mile stretch of beach in ten days. In just that small stretch of beach they collected 7,561 items that weighed 8,554 pounds.

The good news is there are things you can do. The next time you are at the supermarket checkout, say "no" to your loaf of bread being put into another plastic bag. It is actually quite easy to go without using plastic shopping bags altogether. Use a reusable bag, such as a strong cotton or hemp bag, instead.

Always recycle plastic bottles, glass bottles, steel and aluminum cans. Make sure your garbage bin is secured and doesn't let rubbish blow away. Never put chemicals or oil down the drain—they will contaminate rivers and then make its toxic way into our oceans.

Join your local environment group and experience the great satisfaction you will get from making a difference. And if you see a piece of rubbish lying on the footpath, don't step over it—pick it up. It won't get to the bin on its own. If we all do our bit, then one day your kids will also run freely along the seashore, collecting only seashells.

• • •

*Ian Kiernan is Chairman and Founder of Clean Up Australia and Clean Up the World.*

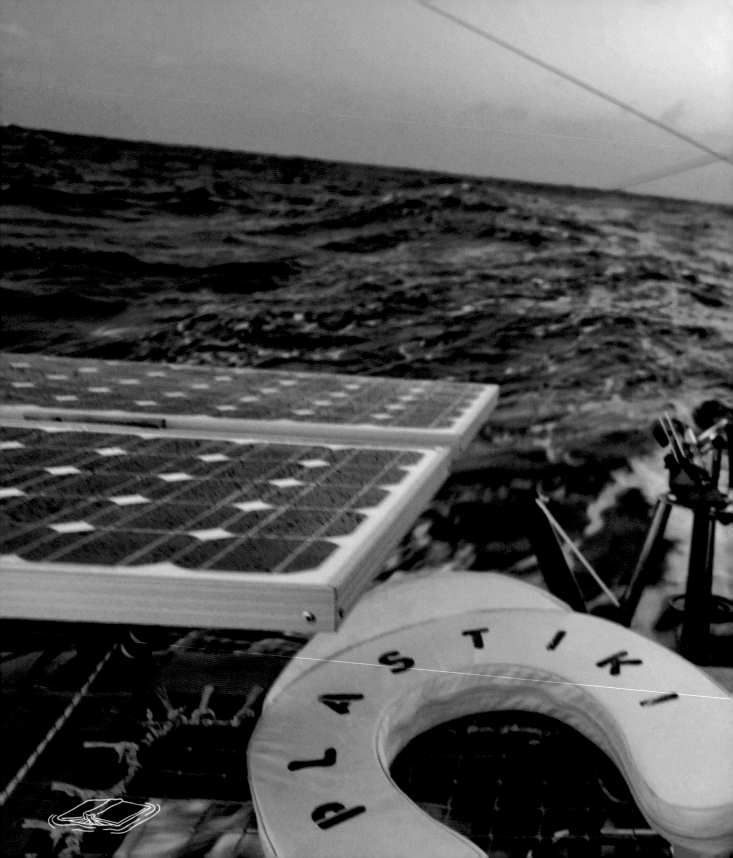

# 6

ADRIFT ON THE BIG, BLUE PACIFIC, MINUTES AND HOURS
WEREN'T THE MEASURE OF A DAY'S PROGRESS SO
MUCH AS THE SUN, THE MOON, AND THE OCEAN'S MOOD.
IN TWENTY-FOUR HOURS, EVERYTHING AND
NOTHING CAN HAPPEN. AND ALL AT ONCE.

# JUNE 25, 2010

**0645** "Morning, David. David, are you awake? Time to get up." Who's shaking me? The only sound I can muster from my desert-dry mouth is more animal than human. My mind has to drag my body from my bunk. After three months of this three-hours-on, three-hours-off sleep routine, you would think the body would have found its rhythm. It hasn't! I scrape the scab on my knee as I get up. You have to be a contortionist or a yogi to get out of this hole unscathed. —David

**0650** The teakettle is whistling as the other watch team walks in, a certain smugness in their tired facial expressions. "Morning, expedition leader! You're in for a treat," says Matt, a bit too enthusiastically. I pass up on a response and make a beeline for the Marmite and some stale and moldy tortilla. —David

**0700** David relieves me at the helm. In the galley, I find somebody has made boiled eggs. I deliriously eat two of them while emptily staring at the blue vastness around me. I head straight for bed. Matt is already in bed.

*Plastiki* is taking huge hits from the waves. This is the most substantial weather we've had the whole trip. It sounds like we're constantly under attack by cannonballs. The boat moans and groans like a wooden warship. This makes sleep a rather ridiculous notion. —Vern

**0710** Cooking up some breakfast, using last night's leftover rice to make rice cakes, eggs, and yummy dried kale. Am about to serve it up but decide a sprinkle of cheese on top would do just the job. On reaching into the cupboard underneath one of the saloon benches, I'm greeted by a whole host of uninvited passengers. Maggots.

Ooowwwooo! One of the jars of beef stew had smashed. There are still some chunks of meat in it, with the remainder of the sauce all over the jars below. My body shivers as I think about reaching in for the broken jar, crawly things all over it!

I quickly forget about the cheese, close the cupboard, and serve breakfast before sharing the news with everyone. We then get to work, boiling pans and pans of hot water, lifting every jar (about one hundred) out of

MAX JOURDAN AT THE TILLER ON AN
AFTERNOON WATCH

**Watch rotates every four days at dinner watch**

| Rotation | WATCH A | WATCH 1 |
|---|---|---|
| 1 | Mr T, Luca, DDR | Jo, Graham, Singeli |
| 2 | Mr T, Luca, Singeli | Jo, Graham, DDR |
| 3 | Mr T, Graham, Singeli | Jo, Luca, DDR |
| 4 | Mr T, Graham, DDR | Jo, Luca, Singeli |
| 5 | MR T, Graham, Luca | Jo, Singeli, DDR |
| 6 | MR T, Luca, DDR | Jo, Graham, Singeli |

| Hour | Day 1 | Day 2 |
|---|---|---|
| 0700 - 1100 | A | 1 |
| 1100 - 1500 | 1 | A |
| 1500 - 1800 | A | 1 |
| 1800 - 1900 | ALL ON WATCH OUTSIDE FOR DINNER | |
| 1900 - 2200 | 1 | A |
| 2200 - 0100 | A | 1 |
| 0100 - 0400 | 1 | A |
| | | 1 |

THE WATCH SYSTEM GAVE EVERY DAY
ON *PLASTIKI* A BASIC SHAPE.

the cupboard, onto deck, and into a line of buckets for cleaning. First step: to be immersed in boiling hot soapy water, next to be wiped, and then scrubbed around the rims with a toothbrush. They're clingy little critters. —Jo

0710 Mine is the top bunk on the starboard side. It's slim but thankfully long, and I can stretch out. I say "mine," but actually it's more Graham's, as he has been the occupant longer than me. We share gracefully, and thankfully not at the same time. "Honey, we probably ought to change our sheets sometime soon," he slipped into the conversation the other day. I had to agree it sounded like a good idea. The truth is that when sleep matters more than anything else, damp mattresses and questionable sheets are bit players in our increasingly primal tendencies. —Matt

0715 I'm lying down with my eyes closed. The cramped bunk, stale air, and jarring and creaking of the boat invariably bring me back to the same place: a Paris-Rome sleeper train nearly twenty years ago. A soothing but uneventful night journey I repeat often aboard the *Plastiki*. It's better than counting sheep, except I never wake up in Italy.

I'm Mum today, and ship rules state I get to sleep the whole night through. I wake at dawn anyway. Apparently it was a rough night, but the noise and waves didn't bother me. I step out on deck and hang over the side in the multicolored ocean glow. —Max

0820 After being at the helm the first hour and twenty minutes, I start hand stitching the seam of the jib back together. The sail tore last night. That's about the fourth time this has happened. —Mr. T

**0850** If you had to design an obstacle course, you'd get pretty high marks for *Plastiki*. Making my way up the pitching boat over the wet plastic deck, I step carefully over the alternately loosening and viciously snapping trip wires connecting the winches to the sails. I duck carefully beneath the loose horizontal ropes attached to the runner, tiptoe through the various metal fittings designed for toe-stubbing, and steady myself with a few grasps for the side of the cabin or the ever-loosening/tightening rope stays. —Graham

**0935** I sit on a jerry can and start to shave. I enjoy the stinging aftershave splash of salt water, and it keeps me grounded. Under a hard sun, the ocean's lost all of its morning subtleties. The sliver of the arcing horizon line is like a cut in the far distance. I go back in, charge some camera batteries, and start to read *The Fountainhead* because it was lying around. Today I can slip out of the routine and *Plastiki* time, but the activity of the crew around me is comforting. We are out here surviving together. A strange community adrift. —Max

**1045** "Wassa weather like?" "Wet." "Wha?" "Wet." "Oh." Graham is eyeing our bed. I dutifully delay him no further and shuffle to the galley for tea. Graham is very good at making tea for the oncoming watch and leaves the cups neatly arranged and ready for collection. I grab a cup and swig fearlessly. Ever the innovator, he has taken to making tea at least twenty minutes before waking us. In that way, he reasons, tea will be ready for gulping without risk of scalding. It's the details that count in this tiny, shrunken world of ours.

"Wet" means wet-weather wear, and judging by the sound of the waves breaking across the deck, I'm gonna need it. The wet-weather wear consists of a large pair of dungaree-style pants and a jacket emblazoned with logos. The thing about the wet-weather wear is that it's always wet, inside and out. Slipping into a wet pair of dungarees is no one's idea of fun. The pants are like a halfway house; they ease you uncomfortably from warm sleeping bag to violent seas. The last piece of the puzzle is the life vest. —Matt

**1050** Our sleep ends. Our watch begins. If you've ever been locked in a grandma's closet with some old fruit, you'd know how the *Plastiki* cabin typically smells. —Vern

**1054** Half a bottle of water (need to drink more water—I always forget), twenty-five songs on the iPod, two splashings by waves later, and I am six minutes away from four hours free to sleep or read. I haven't decided which. Either way, it will be my turn to be smug. I've been at the helm for my favorite time of the day. Wish I could helm all day. This morning's clouds were perfectly aligned with the bow and moving slow enough that I could use them for navigation. Perfect—more space for my brain to fish for ideas. I might go to the front of the boat for a minute while the madness of the watch change subsides. It always feels like the subway at rush hour. —David

**1100** David and I prepare to switch places at the tiller. I clamber across the net, over the tiller and grab hold of the lurching lifeline. I hunker down behind him, salt spray in my eyes. I take the pressure of the tiller and ease it toward me. "Got it?" asks David. "Got it, bruv," I reply. The boat is pitching and rolling violently, waves crashing thunderously beneath us. The cheeriness is part act, part path to a happier place. "Now remember, you got yourselves into this mess, so don't come crying to me," my training sergeant in the armed service loved to chime as we crawled past him in the mud. It's true. We've no one else to blame for the ridiculous situations we get ourselves into.

Whitecaps all around, sprinkled liberally atop the turbocharged swells that roar toward us, towering over the boat until we climb effortlessly up the face, cresting the top and slewing sideways down the back. Settling back down at the helm again, it takes me some time to reestablish the intimacy that I enjoyed with the ocean before handing it over at the end of my last watch. Each time it's different; a different pressure on the tiller, bigger, fatter waves, more or less wind. On each occasion I feel myself descending into a separate zone of consciousness, a sort of elemental chemistry of man and water. —Matt

1135 Most of the eggs seem to have a thick layer of black mold growing on the outside. I can't tell if that means the ones that don't are still okay. General consensus in the cabin is "Don't risk it." Max is Mum today. That means a feast tonight! A bowl of granola will have to fill the gap. —David

1220 On the helm, comfort is of utmost importance since you'll be in this position for at least an hour. For that, you have two options: bumpers or the bags. The bumpers are more solid, made of foam, waterproof, and stackable. They're like an office chair. The bags are floppy, large, and moldable. They're the La-Z-Boy of the nautical world. I'll opt for the bumpers, as the bags have seen better days. They smell of wet socks. The down fibers have begun clumping into balls that tend to drive into the spine, and their original "waterproof" claim seems to have reached the limit. Think wet burrito filled with soggy french fries and golf balls. —Vern

1225 Jo just told me that we are going to need to stop in New Caledonia. Why? I am really not sure this is a good idea. Jo's not listening to my questions or my not-so-subtle pleas. "There is a trough coming in," she throws out in sailor talk. I should have followed Mr. T's lead and gone straight to bed an hour and twenty-five minutes ago. Right now he looks like a tranquilized dog. His mouth is wide open, tongue out. —David

1330 I read most of the day. Hours trickle by to Ayn Rand's rhythm. Around me there is a constant buzz of computers and typing. The cabin feels and hums like an office. We're so connected we are in danger of missing out on the ocean life unfolding around us. Like moths, we're hypnotized by flickering screens, and our solitary and egotistical activities destroy the collective spirit. I get online to check e-mail. I'm as much to blame. —Max

1335 Why am I wet? A wave has just come through my porthole! I am almost too asleep to care. I should get up and sort this out (salt water never dries), but it's an hour and twenty-five minutes until watch again. Try and get back to sleep. Every creak, turn, and bump of the boat contrives against that. —David

1345 It's 97 degrees inside the cabin, so not much chance of any sleep. Read my book for most of my "off watch." —Mr. T

1420 Jo and I had talked about mending the bottles up front. Several of the plastic connectors are broken and will need fixing. To do that I will need to lie down on my front with my head over the side and will need both hands free. I suggest to her that Vern hold my feet. "Okay," she says, "but make sure you wear your life jackets."

"Vern." "Yeessss," he replies, grooming his mustache. Vern has a rakish mustache that he teases out to the sides like a nineteenth-century Texas oilman. "Will you hold my feet while I dangle over the side?" He considers this for a moment and then readily agrees. We monkey walk—center of gravity low and hands out ready to grab onto something—to the front. I'm leaning over the side when the first wave crashes over my head. I try to blow salt water out of my upturned nose, which gives Vern the giggles. I get two cable ties on and maneuver to do the last one. I reach down until I hear an "uh-oh," followed by my being dragged back on deck just in time to

# CREW PROFILE: VERN MOEN

In the annals of sacrificing for one's art, Vern missing the birth of his first child to shoot footage of the *Plastiki* adventure for an upcoming independent film release (scheduled for spring 2011) surely rates up there. Vern's outfit, Long Beach Film Company, specializes in documentaries and music videos for bands such as Cold War Kids, Dead Weather, and Broken Bells. On the *Plastiki* film, Vern is producer, director, shooter, editor.

### WHAT ABOUT LIFE AT SEA SURPRISED YOU MOST?

The desolation. I expected whales, and fish, and dolphins, and other boats—but there was a stretch of time on that first leg where we saw absolutely nothing else other than water and sky. Well, and the other five smelly people on board.

### ARE YOU ON PERMANENT DIAPER DUTY AFTER MISSING THE BIRTH OF YOUR SON?

"Permanent diaper duty" is a euphemism for what I've had to do in an attempt to make it up to my family. It branched out rather quickly to pedicures, chores, and general, familial servitude—all of which I'm trying to oblige.

### WHAT CHALLENGES DID SHOOTING AT SEA PRESENT?

There's the whole, "don't drop your camera in the water" challenge. As well as rust, water, electricity, isolation, solar power/clouds. If something broke— that was it. I had to be prepared for everything, yet everything had to fit into a 1 meter by 1 meter space.

### EVER BEEN SO IMMERSED IN A FILM PROJECT?

This was a tricky, as I had to play the roles of film director and sailor. On big storm days, Jo would come up to me and say "Vern, go help Mr. T bring in the sail." And I'd say, "I can't. I have to film." Which obviously ended with some "negotiating." We settled on, if Jo considered it a substantial safety hazard for me NOT to put on my sailor hat, then I would become sailor.

### FAVORITE PART OF THE DAY ON PLASTIKI?

Going to sleep at 0715 after the 0400-0700 watch.

### LEAST FAVORITE ON-BOARD DUTY?

Waking up.

### WILL YOU EVER AGAIN TAKE FOR GRANTED A QUIET BED?

A "quiet" night's sleep has been redefined. First morning after I returned, I said to my wife, "Boy, William really sleeps, doesn't he?" My wife learned quickly that I need a fist to the arm to wake up now.

MID-OCEAN BOAT CHECKS WERE AN OCCASIONAL TREAT. THE BOTTLES HELD UP WELL AND HOSTED SOME PLANT AND MARINE LIFE.

be met by a huge wave that engulfs us. We are a tangled mess on the deck. We look at each other in surprise. Then, as if on cue, both of our life vests auto-inflate. We burst into laughter as we sit there like two giant orange beetles struggling to find their feet. —Matt

1445 On watch, time is sliced into small increments, making me feel as if I never have time to focus on much of anything except miscellaneous thoughts: The deep blue of the ocean that repeatedly surprises me with its . . . its . . . its blueness. The simple joy at the novelty of collecting rainwater by hooking up the tubes that funnel it from the roof of the cabin into water containers. The calming feeling of running all of our power from the sun and wind. No oil being burned. The guilty feeling of throwing a tin can overboard, even though that's meant to be what we do. —Graham

1524 Back on the helm. Wind is building. Squall clouds closing in. What a pleasure to be out here. The ocean is starting to dance; need to concentrate. The tiller is as heavy as a bag of potatoes; 5.6 knots feels like 20-plus knots. The waves are now smashing up under the belly of *Plastiki*. Bang! Bang! Bang! I can't tell if it's my adrenaline kicking in or a sugar rush from that bag of Gummi Bears I just inhaled. I feel more like I'm sitting on the back of a prize-winning rodeo bull than I do a sailor. The boat is getting lifted and pushed around like a pile of leaves in an autumn gust. "Concentrate, David!" Jo yells. "We need a course of 242 to make New Caledonia!" —David

1556 "Jo! Dave! Sail's ripped!" How did we end up with tissue paper for sails? Waves are building. Need to get downwind. —David

1620 "Stay low and listen! We're going to need to change the sail," shouts Mr. T. "Vern, take over from David. David, grab the storm jib and meet me and Jo up front.

Put some shoes on, and take that iPod off. We're going to need to be quick so as not to tack." I always feel like a tightrope walker whenever I have to go up to the bow. —David

1630 "Grab it. Grab it. Don't let the sail hit the water," shouts Jo. Big wave just hit us. Somehow I managed to stay dry. Not Mr. T. "How do you like that, Mr. T?" I say. "Little wet, are you?" "Karma, mate. Karma," comes the reply. —David

1645 On a normal boat, bringing down a ripped sail and swapping it out for another one would not be such a big deal. But *Plastiki* keeps us hot on our toes, as she will only allow a couple of minutes without flying a headsail before she rounds up into the wind and tacks. Then tacking back is such a big deal. On the way from San Fran to Xmas it once took us five hours to jibe the boat back round! The bows are so narrow it is tricky working two sails at a time up there. Smooth maneuvers, and we were off sailing again in no time. —Jo

1700 New for this leg of the journey is "Power Hour." Well, actually more like half an hour. Think prison yard meets *The Goonies*. Graham, Max, and myself have started a workout routine off the front of the boat. Not the easiest of feats, as the boat is constantly rocking and waves are splashing, but so far our quest for fitness has proven most fulfilling. Workouts include push-ups, sit-ups, sprints on the Dynamo bike, curling with gas cans, pull-ups on the boom, and dips on the beams. Pumping plastic! —Vern

1730 Graham has decided to shave off most of his not insignificant amount of hair. I have clippers, so have volunteered to play barber. The plan is to shave exactly half of Graham's head. This includes his beard, and it makes for an amusing half hour. The wind is blowing across

DAILY LIFE ABOARD PLASTIKI REVOLVED AROUND
MAINTAINING THE RIGGING AND SAILS; FILMING;
SPIRITED CONTESTS OF THE DICE GAME PERUDO;
AND ENDURING THE TEDIUM OF WATCH.

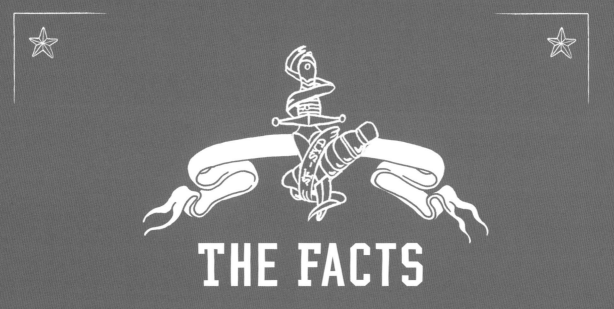

# THE FACTS

70 PERCENT OF THE EARTH'S AVAILABLE OXYGEN
IS PRODUCED BY THE OCEANS.

EACH YEAR, ILLEGAL LONGLINE FISHING KILLS MORE THAN
300,000 SEABIRDS, INCLUDING 100,000 ALBATROSSES.

THE LAST TIME THE EARTH HAD LARGE-SCALE CORAL
DIE-OFFS WAS 11,000 YEARS AGO.

the deck, so we sit him downwind, and I go to work on his hair. Giant lumps whip away in the crosswind. The finished article is odd, a kind of Friar Tuck mullet. It reminds me of brain surgery. —Matt

**1800** Dinnertime. I've knocked out a lamb tagine, a one-pot wonder that can stew until dinner. Served it with brown rice and kale. A well-fed crew is a happy crew. Stomachs and minds. I wolf down my meal before hitting the sack. First night watch only a couple of hours away. —Max

**1815** Max has outdone himself, as usual. But dinner is not the occasion it should be, or could be. The sun is setting. The sky is ablaze with smoking clouds set against a backdrop of the deepest blues studded with early stars. But we're busy, too busy really, to sit, stop, and stare. The watch is changing over. Food is devoured quickly, darkness edges in, the helm is handed over; *Plastiki* slips from day into night. We are thankful to Max for cooking great food, but it's a blip in the day. Many hours' work consumed in a fraction. —Matt

**1835** "I want everyone in their life jackets tonight! If you're on watch, I want you all in your full gear ready to go," commands Jo. Just words to me right now, because I am officially off watch. Another day is over, although I'm not even sure what day of the week it is. I like that. I wish I could take that with me back into the real world. Right now, I am ready for bed. Bang! Another wave hits the underside of *Plastiki*. The deck under my feet buckles upward. I wonder if everyone else is feeling the same as me. Come on, *Plastiki*. Hold in there. Not far now. —David

**2030** "David. David. Sorry, mate, there is a journalist on the phone. BBC Ulster?" —David

**2050** Back on the helm. I double up the bumpers. We're in full weather gear as waves irregularly come crashing over the side. I'm clipped in, and it's a nerve-racking but exciting feeling. —Vern

**2136** Bang, splash. Bang, splash. Another wave crashes down over the roof of the cabin. We're now receiving a consistent barrage of head and body blows. I fumble in the dark to check my porthole. Firmly closed. I feel oddly snug. Through my porthole, I can see Jo's ankle bracelet and her feet tucked under the safety line. Matt is with her. Bang! They have just been swallowed by a wave. That's pretty gnarly. I hope they're both clipped on. —David

**2157** Max just got a massive wave all down his back. Poor guy was just brushing his teeth and was dressed for bed. It's safe to say that this is the biggest sea state, or at least the most violent waves, we've seen. The patched-up storm jib looks like a pirate sail. Keeping on course requires 110 percent concentration. —David

**2245** It's a good night; 20 knots of wind and the stars are out with one bright one right in front of us. Which is great for helming. We have a great watch with speeds of up to 6 knots. —Mr. T

## JUNE 26, 2010

**0100** We are still making great progress, seeing constant speeds of over 5 knots. The best twenty-four-hour run of the whole trip. —Jo

**0230** Night watch. My mind is confused, lost. Reading, helming, a light snack. I found some of Mr. T's chocolate lying around. Don't tell, but I eat some of it. —Vern

**0315** In the spectrum of activity on *Plastiki*, it's been a

A GOOD NIGHT FOR *PLASTIKI:* 20 KNOTS OF WIND
AND THE STARS ARE OUT.

positively exhausting day, and I mercifully retreat into the cabin, leaving Jo and Vern to finish off the helming. Inside, I read a little and exist. I find that there is much existing to be done on *Plastiki*; time filled but not by anything in particular. The very act of existing on *Plastiki* can be an exhausting process, and I congratulate those of the crew who have been existing on the high seas now for more than three months. —Matt

**0350** The only word that comes to mind is *unnatural*. Not the getting-up-at-4-a.m. part, as I have come to peace with that now, but just how much energy I seem to have. Mr. T looks like he is in the same boat. An extraordinary amount of chocolate seems to have just vanished into his mouth. He's out of his bunk like a hare in a trap. He has beaten me to the pole position on the helm. Mr. T seems determined. "Make me a coffee, will ya?" he says. —David

**0415** Wind is still up around 20 knots. Boat's loving it. Then the jib seam blows out on the other sail, and we spend thirty minutes getting down the busted sail and hoisting the sail we had just fixed the day before. —Mr. T

**0630** One of the most spectacular sunrises I have seen all trip. I'm expecting something mystical or magical to come floating down from the rays of sunlight that break through the cloud cover. How lucky and humbling to spend another day on this ocean aboard *Plastiki*. —David

## MESSAGE IN THE BOTTLES

BY PAUL HAWKEN

The voyage of the Plastiki was more than an expedition across an ocean; it was a living allegory that is as much about redemption as are John Bunyan's *Pilgrim's Progress* and James Cameron's *Avatar*, the most popular allegory of all time. The purpose of any parable is to take a metaphor and extend it beyond the narrative, which in this case was the voyage. Like every allegory, David de Rothschild's journey has a literal meaning as well as a symbolic or spiritual meaning.

The literal meaning is specific and vast. The waste we create, seemingly inconsequential in its minutiae—a water bottle here, a plastic bag there...not to worry—is staggering in its entirety. There are nearly a trillion plastic bags made every year and a few hundred billion PET bottles on top of that. Ten percent ends up in the ocean, an invading army that doubles every ten years in quantity and mass. What it does there, we are not sure. We know that it kills marine life through numerous mechanisms, but we don't know the long-term effects of the breakdown products of plastic: antimony trioxide and bisphenol A being two of the most prominent. Plastic does not degrade; it photodegrades in the presence of sunlight and breaks down into smaller and smaller particles, making its ingestion eventually unnoticeable to fish and sea mammals. Plastic that is not consumed or does not become entangled eventually sinks to the bottom of the sea where it will remain for untold centuries.

To make a seaworthy vessel from waste and sail it across a Pacific Ocean plagued by plastic garbage, is the meeting of two paradigms: waste as a nutrient for life or waste as loss of life. It is life or death, depending on whether it is made by living or industrial systems. We are newbie's on the planet, and so is our type of waste. The thermo-industrial system of production makes waste that life forms have never seen before, chemicals and compounds that are put together with such force and manipulation they cannot easily be taken apart. These discards and pollutants are the shadow of our GDP, the unwanted ghost of manufacturing that will visit us far into the future, haunting our oceans, soils, and bloodstreams. The drinks contained in plastic bottles are consumed in minutes but the polymers last for centuries. Commercial carpets are discarded after eight years, but their PVC backing will remain in landfills for 300 centuries. Plutonium waste from nuclear power plants will need to be vigilantly guarded for 2,500 centuries (civilization is about 70 centuries old).

The natural world produces more waste than the debris created by the 6.8 billion people who inhabit the earth, but in nature virtually everything that decays, crumbles, or rots becomes food for detritivores munching in the fecund darkness of soils and oceans. The food we eat depends on the decomposition of the soil beneath it. Life flourishes because waste is nutritious and transient. Nature literally goes to seed. This is a good thing. Nature's waste does not become carcinogenic when it is part of an ecosystem. It does not insert mutagens into pregnant women. It does not concentrate toxins in rusting barrels stored in salt caves. Waste is the last element in the completion of the circle

of life. We need to make good on our waste. This does not mean making boats of water bottles. That is the allegory. The moral is to make our water bodies, our marine bodies, our animal and human bodies taboo to industry. It does not mean we make useful objects of daily life from the world's dumps. It means redesigning civilized life from molecular level, a green chemistry of self-assembled compounds, a non-violent industrialism, one that eschews heavy metals, high heat, pressure, and atomic manipulation so that everything we make is so valuable there are no landfills, so valuable that it would be lunacy to throw it away, anywhere. Ever.

What we are doing, unconsciously but surely, is waging war on nature and ourselves—with the environment as battleground. The Great Pacific Garbage Patch is the modern equivalent of Bunyan's Slough of Despond, one of the graveyards of the war. Sailing thousands of discarded PET bottles lashed together to bring attention to the plastic scum and remnants littering the ocean is a courageous offering, reminding us that nothing can be thrown away—not plastic, people, or places—if we are to live in the truth of the oneness of life. David's voyage contrasts hope and the unforgivable, what could be with what cannot be if we are to uphold this precious life we share as sacred.

• • •

*Paul Hawken is an environmentalist, entrepreneur, and the author of* The Ecology of Commerce, Natural Capitalism, *and* Blessed Unrest.

# 7

## CROSSING THE EQUATOR

AFTER LEAVING CHRISTMAS ISLAND,
*PLASTIKI*'S SLOW-MOTION ISLAND-HOPPING
WAS PUNCTUATED BY A SAILOR'S RITE OF
PASSAGE INVOLVING KING NEPTUNE.

WHEN CAPTAIN JAMES COOK DISCOVERED CHRISTMAS ISLAND IN DECEMBER 1777 DURING HIS THIRD AND FATEFUL VOYAGE INTO THE PACIFIC OCEAN, HE WAS UNDERWHELMED.

He and the crews of his two ships, *Resolution* and *Discovery,* found the island hot, barren, and uninhabited, a far cry from the teeming tropical paradises they routinely stumbled upon. My initial reaction on reaching the atoll was just the opposite—except for the hot part. It's still hot.

Christmas Island today is a beautiful and bustling place full of smiling and incredibly generous people. Every single inhabitant was at the dock in London, the largest town on the island, when we disembarked on April 27. Or maybe it only seemed that way. My case of culture shock after spending thirty-nine days looking at the same five faces was rather extreme.

What I took at first to be a welcoming party of some two hundred people (good organizing, Matt!) proved to be passengers waiting for the ferry *Moa Moa,* their luggage and boxes of fruit piled high. Matt was there to greet us, along with Graham Hill, founder of the environmental Web site treehugger.com, who would join us on the next leg of the journey, and several local officials. There were handshakes all around, and then we were

escorted to a little tent set up off to the side. A small crowd had gathered.

My first steps on land were surreal. After mastering the art of staying upright on the hammock netting at *Plastiki*'s bow and stern and becoming adept at negotiating a lurching, rolling deck cluttered with toe-jamming hazards like coiled rope, winches, cleats, and jerry cans, I was a stranger on terra firma. I don't think I wobbled or staggered, but I could feel my internal gyros and balancing muscles attempting to do a job no longer necessary.

At the tent, we Plastikinauts were handed a delicious bit of irony. Our well-meaning hosts offered us a choice of beverage: a sliced-open green coconut with plastic straw inserted or bottled water. We hemmed and hawed, then all chose the coconut, sans straw. "No straw?" wondered the island official. As we sipped coconut milk, a troupe of five-year-old girls dressed in traditional outfits performed a little dance. It was magical. I made a short speech to the effect that we were humbled and grateful to be on Christmas Island. I did my best to be gracious, though more than anything I craved some

EVERYONE ABOARD *PLASTIKI* TOOK HIS OR HER PLACE AT THE HELM DURING WATCH. HERE, GRAHAM HILL, WHO JOINED ON CHRISTMAS ISLAND, NAVIGATES TOWARD THE EQUATOR.

space. I was frazzled by all of the people and commotion and the intensely pungent smells of smoke, incense, and damp earth.

During the ride in an air-conditioned car to the air-conditioned Captain Cook Hotel, I was struck by two things. First, what a good job humanity does at disconnecting from nature, even when surrounded by an abundance of natural beauty. Second, how wonderfully silent it was in that traveling cocoon.

It turns out *Plastiki* is a loudmouth. She never shuts up. She creaks and squeaks and clicks and groans with every ocean swell. And there's the whoosh of ocean water passing through thousands of plastic bottles. The faster *Plastiki* goes, the louder the whoosh and more pronounced the accompanying vibration. Think of a

WE ARE FINALLY LEAVING XMAS ISLAND! LAND
IS SLIPPING AWAY ON THE HORIZON, AND WE HAVE
A POD OF 40 OR SO DOLPHINS ESCORTING
US SOUTH 2 FIJI!
@DREXPLORE 6:58 P.M., MAY 9, 2010

marching band playing in a cave. I had thought that seasickness or salt sores would be the biggest physical hurdles on this adventure, but they've proven trivial compared with the unrelenting racket aboard our good ship. Several days away from our rackety creation would do me good.

Christmas Island, or Kiritimati, as it's known in the local Gilbertese language, is about as far as you can get on this planet from the major industrial nations, yet it isn't immune to environmental threats. One of a chain of eleven atolls and coral islands, it lies mere feet above sea level, making it a possible casualty if the oceans keep rising. And like many islands in

Micronesia and Polynesia, Kiritimati has a nuclear legacy from British H-bomb testing during the late 1950s.

As I toured the island giving talks before hundreds of high school and middle school students, meeting with local environmental and agricultural groups, and visiting bird sanctuaries and wildlife projects funded by New Zealand and Japan (though in return they're allowed to fish the waters around the island), *Plastiki*'s message of reducing plastic use and increasing recycling efforts fell on receptive ears. We met many friendly people who were enthused about and inspired by *Plastiki*, which in turn inspired us to think about how we can get the message out and have more of an impact. *Kon-Tiki* is very famous there—they actually study it at school—and Olav was a star. So much effort and feeling went into the skits and songs the kids performed. It was very special for all of us.

Part of our stay on Christmas Island was devoted to patching damage inflicted to *Plastiki* as she was towed by motor skiff into the harbor at London. Our local guide professed to be knowledgeable of the lagoon's treacherous shallows but still managed to run our boat aground in 3 feet of water. The damage was minor—some bottles were dislodged and the rudder boxes crushed—but it still took many hours of work to repair, all the while under attack by mosquitoes and the heat. Thirty-nine days and 3,617 miles with nary a blemish were undone in the final few thousand feet to safe harbor.

Preparing *Plastiki* for the next leg of our journey was gritty work. We pulled everything out of the hulls, sponged out the holds, reorganized and repacked the hulls, refilled our giant water bladders, cleaned the galley and living quarters top to bottom, restocked and inventoried our food supply, repaired the mainsail, and greased the mast. Any task involving a local vendor, such as the propane and water suppliers, was certain to take at least twice as long as anticipated. On Christmas, as we discovered, everyone is on island time.

*PLASTIKI* WAS WARMLY WELCOMED ON CHRISTMAS ISLAND, ESPECIALLY BY THE KIDS. RECYCLING WAS APPARENT EVERYWHERE—BUT PLASTIC STILL WINDS UP ON THE BEACH.

# MESSAGES OF SUPPORT

The *Plastiki* expedition had thousands of friends and followers, but none were more important than the many schoolkids who sent in their own wishes and concerns about the oceans. From India to Iran to Australia, their messages of support inspired the crew. These illustrated messages came from McGilvra Elementary School in Seattle, Washington, and included kids' pledges for helping the oceans.

Name Max Baldwin

Dear Plastiki Crew,
My name is Max.
I am going to pick up
trash on 5-29, 30 and 31 ic
at Sandy point.

Name Ria P 5-6-10    May 6 20

Dear Jo.    ster that
ship!!!!!!. My name is
Ria. You rock!
I will help the
environment    look on the back

Name Olivia 5-6-10

Dear Plastiki Crew,
My name is Olivia.
I am going to use
reuseable bags for my
lunch to save the environment
From: Olivia

Name _____

to HELP
the invironment

Dear Plastiki crew,
My name is Ashlyn
am going to turnoff the
sink when I am not using
& I am going to pick up
garbegs

Missing out on all of this fun were Vern, Max, and Olav. Vern had dashed for the airport as soon as we touched land, just barely making the flight to Honolulu. Max took the same flight, bound eventually for Paris, to spend time with his wife and daughter. Olav kicked around Christmas Island for a few days to scuba dive its fantastic reefs and join in any pub crawling before he flew home to Norway. I was sad to see them depart, but also eager to welcome their replacements. Graham Hill, an old friend, founder of treehugger.com, and an engaging and energetic companion, was on the ground on Christmas Island with Matthew Grey several weeks early to help Matt prepare for our arrival. Our longtime photographer, Luca Babini, and our new videographer, Singeli Agnew, would fly in just before we departed.

On the afternoon of May 9, a fully laden *Plastiki* exited the harbor at Christmas Island. We hoisted the mainsail, caught the trade wind, and watched as the palm-fringed coastline faded from view. I was excited to be back at sea and moving on. A pod of forty playful dolphins accompanied us for at least half an hour, leaping at our bow and swimming beneath what for these exquisitely sensitive creatures must have been the strangest-sounding vessel ever. We had received a similar dolphin escort on leaving San Francisco. Ancient Greek mariners interpreted the sight of dolphins playing in a boat's bow wake as a good omen, and that's exactly how I took it.

We had concluded the first phase of our journey and were now embarked for Fiji. Jo calculated our route as a twenty-two-day crossing through the island-studded waters of Polynesia. Spirits on board were running high. We had new crew, new stories to tell, a balmy night on hand, and perfect sailing conditions.

· · ·

THE NON-SAILORS ON *PLASTIKI* CALLED THEMSELVES LAND CRABS—ONLY TO DISCOVER THAT CHRISTMAS ISLAND IS OFTEN OVERRUN BY REAL LAND CRABS.

Finally under way again. It feels so good to be sideways crabbing to the next tropical destination. The plan is Fiji, but as you know, the good lady *Plastiki* has a life of her own, so we can but will her to Fiji with no high expectations of speed or final destination!

For a moment there, it felt like she wanted to stay in Kiritimati. On our day of departure, the local wind whistled up more than we had seen it throughout our stay. It took a lot of laying various anchors and winching our way around through the strong headwind and around the coral heads to finally escape. A little like the old schooner days.

It was really exciting to share Graham and Singeli's first night at sea under the tropical starry night. They have really taken to life at sea and are feeling great. The vibe on board is wonderful.

·······················

"Three. Two. One. Zero. Whooo, whooo."

The LCD display on the boat's GPS unit flashed 00°00.000' in latitude. *Plastiki* had crossed the equator, leaving behind the Northern Hemisphere and entering the Southern. Of course, nothing really changed by crossing the invisible line. The setting sun still dropped quickly toward the horizon. The night's first stars, now glimmering in the east, held the same alignment as last night. But everyone on board sensed the significance of the moment.

"In a spiritual sense, crossing the equator gives sailors a chance to be thankful, traditionally to Neptune, the God of the Sea," explained Jo in prepping us earlier. She is a veteran of three equatorial crossings. "In my mind, you are in a special place—where all the energies from the north meet the south—to thank Mother Earth for the life support she selflessly offers and ask for forgiveness for the harm we have caused the oceans since our last crossing."

At the appointed time, each of us took a position at the edge of the boat and conducted a private invocation. Given that we were on a mission to help Neptune, the event seemed especially meaningful. I had written a note thanking Neptune for safe passage and expressing hope that the *Plastiki* project lessens the impacts on the ocean. I carefully folded the piece of paper and tossed it into the water. Jo threw a stone, Luca a bandanna, Mr. T a dram of rum, Graham a vitamin pill, and Singeli a piece of chocolate.

With that we cracked open a bottle of warm champagne and enjoyed a delicious dinner in celebration. Amid the merriment, I had a sneaking suspicion we weren't yet done in fulfilling the traditions of an equatorial crossing. Graham felt the same way. I'd heard from several friends about ritual hazing of first timers. Jo and Mr. T's snickering and sly glances early the next morning confirmed my fears.

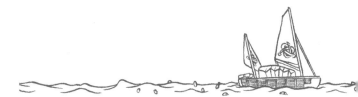

CROSSED THE EQUATOR TIED UP, BLINDFOLDED, BEING SCOLDED BY NEPTUNE AND COVERED IN KITCHEN SLOP. MY LIFE IS STRANGE SOMETIMES.
@GHILL 2:06 P.M., MAY 12, 2010

"Wake up, Pollywogs. Wake up!" Mr. T yelled as he ran through the cabin banging on a pot. It seemed Jo and Mr. T had been replaced by Neptunus Rex and her first assistant, Davy Jones. Mr. T, as a gender-confused Davy Jones, was dressed in a short turquoise sarong, with a coconut-shell bra, an orange headdress, and shell jewelry. We four Pollywogs, or maiden equator crossers, were blindfolded and tied together on deck. "Neptune's Revenge" was upon us. We were taking

# CONSUMING THE PLANET

Selling ice to Eskimos. That's the genius of corporate marketers. After all, they've convinced people the world over to pay ten thousand times more for a bottled version of a product that flows out of the tap at home. According to Lester Brown, president of the Earth Policy Institute and author of *Plan B 4.0*, our manipulated desires are getting the better of us and the natural systems that must satisfy them.

### THE AVERAGE PERSON HAS NO IDEA HOW HIS SHOPPING HAS ANY BEARING ON THE ENVIRONMENT. HOW IS THAT?

One of the things we don't include are the externalized costs. When we burn coal, we pay the costs of mining coal, getting it to the power station, and delivering the electricity, but we don't pay the cost of treating respiratory illness from breathing coal pollution, and we certainly don't pay the cost of climate change. Not paying the indirect costs is symptomatic of our entire economy. The policy tool that I would use to get the market to tell the environmental truth would be tax restructuring: lowering income taxes and offsetting that with a carbon tax.

### IS THE PACE OF TECHNOLOGICAL CHANGE IN PERSONAL ELECTRONICS AND THE WASTE IT GENERATES A CONCERN?

Yes, it's a major source of waste. Some countries are requiring that computers be designed to be disassembled and the various components recycled. Nokia, the cell-phone maker, has a phone you can disassemble in a matter of seconds. That's the kind of mind-set we need.

### CAN THE EARTH AFFORD BILLIONS MORE PEOPLE CONSUMING AT THE LEVEL OF AMERICANS AND EUROPEANS?

The fossil fuel–based, car-centered, throwaway economy is not a viable option for the future for anyone. For China, instead of blindly adopting the Western industrial model that evolved during the last two centuries, why not ask the question, What would an economy designed for the twenty-first century look like? It will be powered by wind, solar, and geothermal. It will be very sensitive to land scarcity. It will be very much aware of water scarcity.

### HAVE WE REACHED THE POINT OF OUTSTRIPPING THE SUSTAINABLE YIELD OF OUR NATURAL SYSTEMS?

Yes, probably around 1980 we passed that. We're probably about 30 percent beyond that, according to the calculating method used by Matthis Wackernegel, president of the Global Footprint Network.

### HOW MUCH TIME DO WE HAVE TO TURN THIS AROUND?

It's clear to me that if we stay with business as usual, we're toast. The question is, "When does this happen?" It may be that it's already started to happen and we just don't realize it, just as with the Mayas, Sumerians, and Easter Islanders. The World Bank estimates that 175 million Indians are being fed with grain produced by overpumping water from aquifers. There are a number of other countries that are overpumping extensively, too. So you have artificially inflated food production.

### WHAT CAN ONE PERSON DO?

I think people expect me to say, "Change your lightbulbs," "Recycle your newspapers." Those things are important. But we've got to change the system. We have to accelerate the shift of fossil fuels for renewables. And that means restructuring the tax system. It's about becoming politically active. What's at stake now is civilization itself.

THE CORE CREW AFTER CHRISTMAS ISLAND, FROM LEFT TO RIGHT: SIGNELI AGNEW, LUCA BABINI, DAVID DE ROTHSCHILD, GRAHAM HILL, DAVID THOMSON, AND JO ROYLE.

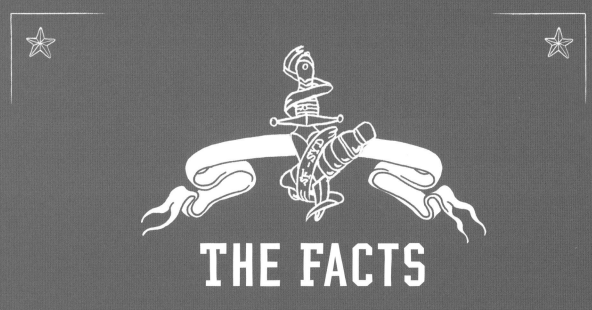

# THE FACTS

MORE THAN 85 MILLION PLASTIC BOTTLES
ARE USED EVERY THREE MINUTES.

BOTTLED WATER COSTS 1,900 TIMES MORE PER GALLON THAN TAP.

IN TASTE TESTS, LONDON TAP WATER BEAT 20 BRANDS OF
BOTTLED WATER, AND NEW YORK CITY TAP WATER BEAT OUT
EVIAN AND POLAND SPRING.

part in a venerable tradition; sailors the world over are dragged before King Neptune's court to seek forgiveness and initiation into the ranks of the Shellbacks.

"Landlubbers, your captain asked you to seek forgiveness for the sins committed against the ocean, but I, King Neptune, feel we have weak-minded Pollywogs on board. Weak!" cried Jo, wearing a ridiculous cardboard crown and beard. "A punishment is in order before these Pollywogs can be blessed with the title of Shellback, showing that forgiveness had been granted. What say you, Davy?"

"I think they need some slops," Davy Jones declared. That would explain the bucket of soupy kitchen swill Mr. T had been cooking in the sun yesterday. With that, ladles of vomitous liquid were poured over our heads.

"What is this?" I sputtered.

"I would keep your mouth closed," replied Mr. T, barely able to suppress retching himself.

"Lord and master of the world's oceans and seas, King Neptune grants his forgiveness," said Jo.

In the days to follow, it was difficult to figure out whether Neptune had been appeased. For one glorious evening, the wind aligned perfectly with a smooth sea to allow us the rare opportunity to fly the spinnaker. The quiet that comes with having a kite up versus a mainsail allowed for deep slumber. Other times, massive thunderstorms rolled through, especially at night. Lightning bolts crackled across the entire night sky. With the lightning came rain the likes of which I'd never seen. It would rain and rain for hours, rain so hard it was like being pelted by a truckload of water balloons. During these tempests, I'd look at the aluminum mast, so fat, so upright, so metallic, and think, "That has PLEASE COME AND STRIKE ME written all over it." Fortunately, the lightning chose other targets. One key distinction we noticed upon entering the Southern Hemisphere was an increase in sea life. The water teemed with schools of small fish. We'd occasionally look down only to see

an eyeball staring right back from below the surface: big squid. They were everywhere. After the scarcity of the Northern Hemisphere, all of the marine life made the ocean seem neighborly.

THE HEAT AND SLEEPLESSNESS BECAME CRIPPLING TO OUR PHYSICAL AND MENTAL STATES. MY SKIN WAS CRACKING ALL OVER, AND I HAD SOME PRETTY NASTY SALT SORES TO BOOT.

In the wake of the storms, the wind would die and the temperature soar. One day we averaged 2.5 knots per hour, the next just 1.2 knots. On a few occasions, the life buoy we trailed would float past the boat, meaning we were basically at a standstill, and the buoy, being lighter, would float past as if to say, "Look at me; I can move faster than you!" During the day, the cabin became a sweat lodge. It was impossible to remain inside for more than a few minutes at a go. Outside wasn't much better. The decking baked in the tropical sun until it became painful to the touch. We built elaborate awnings to try to hide from the sun. At night, those of us off watch would bring our bedding outside to try to sleep while suspended in the cargo netting near the bow. The lifeboat was also a favorite place for people to sleep. Invariably we were chased back inside by the next squall.

The heat and sleeplessness became crippling to our physical and mental states. My skin was cracking all over, and I had some pretty nasty salt sores to boot. Sheets of skin were peeling off of Graham's hands. It was physically a very testing time for the team, perhaps more so for Singeli and Luca, who had come straight from balmy San Francisco. Graham at least had been on Christmas Island a few weeks to acclimatize to the heat

# CREW PROFILE: GRAHAM HILL

Good company is essential on any adventure, and they don't come more engaging or energetic than Graham Hill. Graham, an architect by training and self-described "designpreneur," has started companies in fields as diverse as skateboarder clothing, Web site development, and manufacturing a souvenir ceramic Greek coffee cup. He also founded treehugger.com, one of the Web's busiest eco-focused sites. Now he's launching twenty-four-hour cable station Planet Green with Discovery Communications. Graham's a weekday vegetarian and an avid kiteboarder.

### WHY PLASTIKI AND NOT A CARNIVAL CRUISE VACATION?

*Plastiki* is bright red, Carnival Cruise a dull beige. One has a cause; one doesn't. One gets around with a free source of power; the other by burning oil.

### COULD YOU KITEBOARD TO AUSTRALIA FASTER THAN PLASTIKI?

With a chase boat to sleep on and to hole up in when there isn't any wind, certainly! Probably a whole lot faster.

### DONE MUCH SAILING BEFORE?

Bits here and there. A lot of kiting.

### WHAT TURNED YOU INTO AN ENVIRO?

Hippie parents?

### GOT ANY ENVIRONMENTAL PEEVES?

Bottled water and filet mignon hors d'oeuvres served at environmental events. If we can't even get the little things right in a very public setting, how are we ever going to get the big picture right?

### SINGLE BIGGEST THING ANYONE CAN DO TO SAVE THE PLANET?

Understand what your carbon footprint is composed of and focus on reducing the larger parts of it.

### MOTTO YOU LIVE BY?

If you don't ask, the answer is always "no."

### BEST PART OF THE DAY ON PLASTIKI?

Good, fast sailing with larger waves. And dinner.

### FAVORITE THING ABOUT THE OCEAN?

Big, wild, and mysterious. I love zooming around on top of it, jumping off of things into it, lolling around in it, and scuba diving deep in it.

### WHAT ARE YOU READING?

I've read a ton of books on board, but I'm currently reading *The Brothers Karamazov*, by Dostoyevsky. I am trying to read more classics.

### WHAT'S NEXT AFTER PLASTIKI?

Getting back to New York to work on my tiny, ultra-green renovation.

THE PACIFIC OCEAN PROVED TO BE VERY
UNPREDICTABLE, WITH THE SKY QUICKLY
CHANGING TO OMINOUS STORM CLOUDS.

and humidity. The thing that kept us going was a dark, aromatic brew prepared by our crazy Italian, Luca. He fed us pot after pot of the best Italian coffee anyone had tasted, made with the flair of a master painter stroking the canvas.

"The adventure of the mind is taken to a whole different level!" said Jo of our predicament.

Spirits on board were amazingly good. Everyone was cheerful about chipping in with duties, eager to converse, and at the same time respectful of each other's need for space and solitude. There was a much more relaxed feeling than on the first leg. I ascribe a lot of that to crew selection and how steep the learning curve on *Plastiki* was on the first leg. After Christmas Island, we had a routine down—though we soon found ourselves telling new teammates what to do and how to act. We'd become boring old hands! Not cool!

Deciding who joins an expedition is really more intuition than science. You want people who are enthusiastic, have special skills, and bring something to the game with their attitude and storytelling. Egomaniacs need not apply. My rule of thumb is: If you don't get along with someone on land, you definitely won't on an expedition.

Social scientists are fascinated with how the human psyche functions when a small group is isolated from the rest of humanity, forced into cramped quarters, and subjected to extreme environments in which hazards abound. The focus of the scientists' attention has been on astronauts spending prolonged periods in space and people who work at Antarctic research stations through the long, dark winter. In many respects, the living conditions on *Plastiki* didn't seem all that different. Predictably, what the scientists have found is that relationships strain and become a huge source of stress. Compound that with the inability to get away from the person or situation. Some individuals snap in violent ways under the tension, set off by the tiniest tic or comment. More typically, groups subdivide into factions that play out us-versus-them grudges.

As stressful as deep isolation can be, it does have its positive aspects. By stripping away distracting stimuli so numerous in everyday life that we don't even register them—ringing phones, barking dogs, humming computers—personal breakthroughs can be achieved. Sensory reduction induces an almost meditative state leading to vivid dreams, deep relaxation, and an ability to let go of habits like overeating, smoking, and drinking. Which would explain my success in a bet I made with my brother—that he'd greet me in Sydney with an ice-cold beer if I didn't touch a drop for the entire voyage. I'm proud to say I won that beer!

Fortunately, our crew on the second leg of the journey displayed no interpersonal strife. Perhaps the addition of Singeli had something to do with it, as researchers examining human dynamics in inhospitable conditions find that teams composed of men and women function more smoothly. Certainly some of the credit goes to our reconfigured watch system. We continued to adhere to the three-hours-on, three-hours-off format but with a twist. Rather than stick to two teams with the potential to go all tribal, we rotated individuals through teams on a daily basis. We'd learned our lesson from the first leg, on which relations broke down to the point that Mr. T and Olav hardly ever spoke to each other. I tried to mediate that cold war, but to no avail. What's curious is that as soon as Mr. T and Olav landed on Christmas Island, they got along like a house afire and became inseparable.

THE UNEXPECTED WIND, PLASTIKI IN HER ELEMENT AT 6 KNOTS! RIDE ON, WIND IN THE HAIR, WAVES ON THE HEAD!
@JO_ROYLE 8:00 P.M., MAY 21, 2010

### CREW VIEW: LUCA BABINI

We sail a petrol ocean that we can't see in a moonless, balmy night. The sea is resting after a day of heavy sparring, with blows coming from all sides and sharp winds. It feels like we are the weight at the end of a pendulum hooked to the sky. The Milky Way is close enough to take a bite at it. Stars wait for their turn to fall at the beginning of Galaxy's runways. So many are crossing the sky that you quickly run out of loved ones to make wishes for.

While sailing the big blue desert that is the Pacific, we warmly received any visitor. On several occasions, frigate birds, the long-distance pilots of the ocean, attempted to catch a breather by roosting on our mast. Their fluttering attempts at landing absorbed everyone's attention; their failure left us a bit dejected when the birds flew off. A pod of pilot whales trailing in our wake excited and delighted the whole crew. The same applied to the giant ocean-crossing freighters that would occasionally cross our path. I made a bit of a sport out of trying to strike up a conversation over the VHF radio even though it's a breach of mid-ocean protocol.

"Hello, this is *Plastiki*," I spoke into the handset to a huge tanker a mile off our starboard. "Do you see us?"

"Yeah, I do," came the reply.

"Where you going?"

"I'm off to Japan."

"How long will that take?"

"Should be there in thirteen days."

"Have you got any ice cream on board you could spare?"

"Uh, negative."

Most of the pilots either wouldn't respond or barely spoke English. With one Indian pilot, I attempted a more substantive dialogue.

## KICKING THE HABIT

Nine teams in the 2010 World Cup soccer tournament sported jerseys and shorts made by Nike out of recycled plastic bottles. Each jersey contains the equivalent of eight plastic bottles, melted down and spun into soft, lightweight, and breathable polyester thread. Making the shirts for the teams and their fans consumes 30 percent less energy than using raw materials, says Nike, and will divert 13 million bottles from landfills in Japan and Taiwan. All good, right? Not exactly. Since the jerseys won't ultimately get recycled, they are a prime—though colorful—example of "downcycling." Saved from the landfill, the plastic in the uniforms, when worn and faded, will someday end up there.

"We're a boat made of plastic bottles that's trying to get people to reduce the amount of plastic they dispose in the oceans," I said by way of introduction.

"Oh, that's nice."

"Plastic pollution is killing marine wildlife and entering the food chain."

"I'm about to have dinner."

"Do you know how much plastic ends up in the ocean?"

"Ah, no, but I'll look it up while I'm eating my dinner. I really must go now."

As we headed southwest toward Fiji, it became clear that *Plastiki* was sagging farther to the south than we wanted. Once again, our vessel's sideways drift was coming into play. Untold hours at the tiller had taught us that not only does *Plastiki* have a narrow window for optimal wind direction, she's also picky about wind speed. Above 12 knots per hour, the boat tracks reasonably well. Below 12 knots, she navigates about as well as a jellyfish. In a normal weather year, slack winds wouldn't be an issue. The trades blow strongly and consistently. But, as previously noted, 2010 was the year of an abnormally strong El Niño weather pattern, which had disturbed wind flows across the Pacific. We would have considered ourselves lucky with a wind speed of 12 knots.

"I just checked the weather, and we have this same wind forecast for the next six days," reported Jo. Straight ahead of us lay the Samoan island of Upolu. Jo pored over the charts to figure out whether we would skirt the island to its east or to the west. Forty-eight hours before we sailed right into Upolu, I turned to Jo and said, "Why don't we just stop in Samoa? Why go to Fiji?"

The arguments for and against stopping in Samoa were a bit of a toss-up. In the negative, Matt, who had been on Fiji for several weeks meeting with government officials and taking care of logistics, would be forced to relocate. And the last leg of the journey into Australia,

ON GOOD DAYS, *PLASTIKI* COULD MAKE 6 OR 7 KNOTS, AND THE BEAUTY AND SPIRIT OF THE VOYAGE BUOYED EVERYONE'S SPIRITS.

arguably our most challenging, would grow from twenty days to more than thirty-five days. In the positive column, stopping in Samoa set us up advantageously for the final push to Australia. We would have the choice to go around New Caledonia either to its north, using the island as a shield against wintry low-pressure systems hurtling up from Antarctica, or to its south, on a more direct but more exposed route. Sailing to Fiji, on the other hand, we'd be locked into sailing south of New Caledonia.

"Samoa it is," declared Jo.

We were just twelve days removed from Christmas Island, having sailed 1,866 miles—a good 800 miles shy of our intended goal—when Samoa's big, lush green hills burst through the blue. It seemed *Plastiki* wanted to come straight here. She had a calling, and we obliged. Maybe she knew something we didn't. On Samoa we would discover a critical structural failure that might have doomed the boat, the mission, and us.

## ISLANDS ARE "NATURAL NETS" FOR PLASTIC-CHOKED SEAS

### BY MARCUS ERIKSEN

I stood on the shore in Waveland, Mississippi, pointing to the streams where I caught catfish and blue crabs when I was a kid.

My stepfather was a fisherman. I said to my wife, "There were houses here." My stepfather and the house are now gone, the neighborhood leveled by Hurricane Katrina.

Walking to the beach, blobs of rust-colored oil glisten from the Gulf oil spill. A confetti of torn bits of colored plastic, polystyrene, and plastic pellets litter the space between them along the water's edge. It wasn't this way before. I haven't spent this much time here in twenty-five years. I've seen the baseline shift.

This is a tale of two oil spills. Plastic floating in the five subtropical gyres of the world and the Gulf spill are two petroleum disasters.

From each barrel of oil, 8 percent becomes plastic: 4 percent is the raw material, 4 percent is the fuel to power the process. It is nonbiodegradable and lasts virtually forever, yet we make products from it to be thrown away.

Plastic has been entering our seas for fifty years. The 5 Gyres Project has recently crossed the North Atlantic Gyre and Indian Ocean Gyre.

I've twice studied the North Pacific Gyre with Captain Charles Moore of the Algalita Marine Research Foundation. These oceans, and the fish that live there, are full of plastic that has been reduced to confetti. The plastic is incessant from shore to shore, spread out like a spoonful of sand across a football field—over two-thirds of the earth's surface.

You cannot clean up the gyres by going to the gyres. "Trying to clean up the Pacific gyre would bankrupt any country and kill wildlife in the nets in the process," Moore recently said.

It's much like smog in Los Angeles, a small particulate dispersed over a large area. Some had suggested putting filters on top of skyscrapers to filter air pollution from the clouds, but they were met with laughter. People could see smog and recognize that treating the symptom was impractical, so we treated the source with better engines and catalytic converters inside mufflers. It worked. The smog lifted.

Going to the gyres with boats and barges capitalizes on the public's misconception that there are Texas-sized islands of plastic. Although you may find a few tangled nets, buckets, and bottle caps, there are no fabled islands of trash, only a thin soup of plastic.

You can't go and get the plastic in the five gyres, but you can wait for it to come to you. Hawaii, Oahu, Bermuda, the Azores, the Galápagos, and Mauritius are natural nets sitting in the path of gyre currents.

In time, the five gyres will kick debris onto their shores, at low cost or no cost, with a low carbon footprint, and with no death to marine life in the process. The plastic will leave the gyres as long as we stop adding more.

Long-term solutions will treat the source, not the symptom. Three steps will do it.

First, "benign by design" is a call to the producers to use green chemistry to change the material to be inert in the environment. New bioplastics, like PHA from Metabolix, looks, feels, and acts like plastic but is marine bio-degradable.

Second, "cradle to cradle" is a call to manufacturers to assume responsibility for the end game of what we make, building in a recovery plan for every widget. By extending producer responsibility to the full life cycle, there is no concept of waste. Cradle to cradle is also a call to the consumer to eliminate waste with smart consumer choices. Before you buy, think ahead to the life cycle of the product and its package.

Third, "laws to level the playing field" is a call to lawmakers and the public to give innovation a fighting chance. Many companies want to use alternative materials and design, but the bottom line is cost. Legislation creates fairness in the marketplace.

It is important that we remove the plastic waste that is washing ashore on islands in the gyres. But we must also turn off the tap of waste flowing into our oceans. Our ocean, the land that washes down to her, and the people who earn their sustenance from the sea deserve this change.

• • •

*Marcus Eriksen is an environmentalist and cofounder of the 5 Gyres Project.*

# 8

STATE OF THE OCEANS

THE STARK TRUTH ABOUT THE OCEANS IS THAT
THEY ARE TERRIBLY DAMAGED. OVERFISHING
HAS LAID WASTE TO WHOLE SPECIES; EXCESS
CO2 IS CHANGING THE BASIC CHEMISTRY OF
OUR WATERS; AND GLOBAL WARMING
IS KILLING CORAL REEFS.

FORGET SAMOA—LET'S HEAD FOR THE GULF! AS NEWS OF OIL SPURTING INTO
THE SEA OFF THE COAST OF LOUISIANA REACHED US, AND THE SIZE
OF THE SPILL GREW WITH EACH PASSING DAY, ALL OF THE WORLD
TOOK NOTICE. CONCERN TURNED TO OUTRAGE.

And we were frustrated on *Plastiki*. Here we were on a mission to raise awareness of the threats to the sea, and we were thousands of miles away from an unfolding catastrophe.

Three months later, when the out-of-control well was finally capped, 206 million gallons of crude oil had been released into the gulf, making it the largest accidental spill in U.S. history. Considering the extent of the spill, the immediate death toll to sea life was minimal, and damage to marshes and beach relatively contained.

Even in the face of an ecological disaster, our capacity for delusion is startling. As we watched the news coverage in snippets on *Plastiki,* the media at times seemed more concerned with the effects of the spill on BP's stock value than on its effects to ecosystems. Also, rarely if ever during the crisis did we gain the perspective that as bad as spills like BP's assuredly are, many times more oil washes into North American waters from leaking autos, sloppy oil changes, and leaking underground storage tanks every year than the *Exxon Valdez* spilled in Prince William Sound.

Not to mention the dire damage from less-regulated oil industries in places like Nigeria.

I think the ocean's size and mystery are the root of the problem. After sailing across the Pacific for four months, I still had a difficult time wrapping my head around how big the Pacific is. I also witnessed the ocean in all its majesty and brutal intimidation. The ocean preoccupied my every thought, it seeped into every inch of my imagination, and it became infused into every fiber of my being. And yet I was still wary of it. I learned to read its subtleties and many moods. My understanding couldn't possibly approach that of the original Polynesian sailors, who intuited from shifts in currents, or wave shape and movement, or the direction of the wind, exactly what to expect of the ocean. But I knew enough to hold the utmost respect for it.

Living on the ocean was like being in a cage with an 800-pound gorilla. Its mood was unpredictable, changing from placid and beautiful to snarling and scary in an instant. The ocean, like that gorilla, is so insanely powerful that while it might not mean to harm us, it could

OVERFISHING AND OTHER DESTRUCTIVE PRACTICES HAVE DECIMATED THE MARINE LIFE HUMANS DEPEND ON. SOME FISH ARE ESSENTIALLY GONE; OTHERS ARE ON THEIR WAY.

crush us with barely a flick of its finger. To survive, we had to be aware and nimble and think ahead. Which is precisely what we humans neglect in our relationship to the ocean. We fantasize that the ocean's bounty is limitless, that we can keep taking without putting back. Reality tells a different tale.

• • •

The whine of the fishing reel took everyone by surprise. For the two weeks since departing San Francisco, we had dangled a garish, fluorescent lure behind the boat in what had become an empty gesture. Where were all of the fish? We hadn't seen a single specimen, large or small.

The line had nearly played out by the time Max was able to grab the rod and put his weight behind it. The rod bent in half. "Feels like I'm dragging an oil drum," he shouted.

"If you get tired, I can take over," said Olav a little too eagerly. In his hand was the wooden truncheon he'd been carving all week.

"I hope we haven't caught a shark," said Max.

It took a while, but the fish gave up the fight. Together, Max and Olav hauled aboard a flashing silver, blue, and yellow monster. Olav declared it the biggest tuna he'd ever caught.

For the next three days, we feasted on steaks and fillets for breakfast, lunch, and dinner, until we couldn't stomach another bite. The fish was delicious, but I had a gnawing ambivalence about our bounty. I couldn't help thinking of the dire situation in our empty seas. It's easy to be seduced by the size of the oceans into thinking that their yield is boundless, that another tuna will soon take the bait.

One of the things that struck me about the *Kon-Tiki* expedition is the bountiful sea life the team encountered on nearly every one of their 101 days at sea. From the moment the boat tapped into the Humboldt Current

until it crash-landed on Raroia, creatures large and small were constant companions. Thor Heyerdahl wrote of a passing school of dorado so big it churned the sea surface as far as the eye could see in every direction. Pods of whales swam at the raft at ramming speed, only to duck beneath it at the last possible moment. Sharks were so numerous that the crew feared swimming and took to grabbing and hauling aboard six-foot and larger sharks by their tails for entertainment. Fish was on the menu every night and no more trouble to catch than tossing a baited squid into the water and waiting a minute or two for a bonito or dorado to latch on.

At night, the denizens of the deep surfaced to check out *Kon-Tiki*. Gigantic whale sharks, as many as three at a time and each coated in glowing phosphorescence, glided beneath the humble craft in an eerie dance that would last for hours. The night watch would occasionally be spooked by the light of the lantern dangling from the stern of the boat reflecting off of unblinking, basket-

INSTEAD OF AN AQUATIC WONDERLAND, WE SAILED A BLUE DESERT. I CAN COUNT ON ONE HAND OUR ENCOUNTERS WITH WILDLIFE.

ball-sized eyeballs, which were presumed to belong to giant squid. In the morning, the duty of the first person up was to toss back the baby squid and fry up all of the flying fish that had landed on the bamboo decking overnight. The ocean was abundant, and it was generous.

Our experience aboard *Plastiki* was, tragically, the exact opposite. Instead of an aquatic wonderland, we sailed a blue desert. I can count on one hand our encounters with wildlife: the pod of pilot whales that chased us as we neared Christmas Island; our dolphin escorts; and the frigate bird or two that attempted to

# THERE'S NOTHING TASTY ABOUT SHARK-FIN SOUP

It's hard to love a killer, but sharks could use a few friends. Between 73 million and 100 million of these predators are being slaughtered annually to satisfy the growing demand for shark fin-soup in Asia's thriving economies.

In China, Hong Kong, Taiwan, and elsewhere in the region, shark-fin soup is a status symbol once reserved for elites but now in demand by the region's expanding middle class. At a price of up to $150 a bowl, shark-fin soup served at weddings and other ceremonies signals newfound wealth.

Shark fin can fetch $500 a pound, which has unleashed a worldwide fishing frenzy for most varieties of shark. It's common practice for fishermen to butcher the fin from live sharks and then toss the wounded fish overboard. Without its fin, a shark can't swim, so it sinks to the bottom and endures a slow, painful death.

For the sake of human vanity, an apex species in the ocean food chain—and as a result, marine ecosystems dependent on sharks—is in peril. (Imagine the havoc in Africa if we eradicated big cats.) Shark populations are down 70 percent in the past three decades, with whitetip sharks leading the way toward extinction with a 99 percent decline.

The cruel irony is that shark fin is a chewy, flavorless hunk of cartilage. In June 2010, Hawaii became the first jurisdiction to ban the sale of shark-fin soup and criminalize the possession or sale of shark fins. The nonprofit conservation group WildAid is leading a campaign to end the sale of shark-fin soup that includes TV spots and billboards featuring NBA star Yao Ming.

# MAKE OCEAN-FRIENDLY SEAFOOD CHOICES

If you enjoy seafood, the Monterey Bay Aquarium's Seafood Watch guides are a great way to ensure you're eating as sustainably as possible. "Best Choices" are abundant, well managed, and caught or farmed in ecofriendly ways. "Good Alternatives" are an option, but there are concerns with their harvest or their habitat. "Avoid" means avoid for now: these fish are overfished or harvested in harmful ways. Learn more at montereybayaquarium.org.

| BEST CHOICES | GOOD ALTERNATIVES | AVOID |
|---|---|---|
| Arctic Char (farmed) | Caviar, Sturgeon (U.S. farmed) | Caviar, Sturgeon* (imported wild) |
| Barramundi (U.S. farmed) | Clams (wild) | Chilean Seabass/Toothfish* |
| Catfish (U.S. farmed) | Cod: Pacific (U.S. trawled) | Cobia (imported farmed) |
| Clams (farmed) | Crab: Blue*, King (U.S.), Snow | Cod: Atlantic, imported Pacific |
| Cobia (U.S. farmed) | Flounders, Soles (Pacific) | Flounders, Halibut, Soles (Atlantic) |
| Cod: Pacific (Alaska longline) | Herring: Atlantic | Groupers* |
| Crab: Dungeness, Stone | Lobster: American/Maine | Lobster: Spiny (Brazil) |
| Halibut: Pacific | Mahi-Mahi/Dolphinfish (U.S.) | Mahi-Mahi/Dolphinfish (imported) |
| Lobster: Spiny (U.S.) | Oysters (wild) | Marlin: Blue*, Striped* |
| Mussels (farmed) | Pollock (Alaska wild) | Monkfish |
| Oysters (farmed) | Salmon (WA wild)* | Orange Roughy* |
| Sablefish/Black Cod | Sablefish/Black Cod (CA, OR, | Salmon (CA and OR* wild) |
| (Alaska or BC) | and WA) | Salmon (farmed, incl. Atlantic)* |
| Salmon (Alaska wild) | Scallops: Sea | Sharks*, Skates |
| Scallops (farmed off-bottom) | Shrimp (U.S., Canada) | Shrimp (imported) |
| Shrimp: Pink (OR) | Squid | Snapper: Red |
| Striped Bass (farmed or wild*) | Swai, Basa (farmed) | Swordfish (imported)* |
| Tilapia (U.S. farmed) | Swordfish (U.S.)* | Tilapia (Asia farmed) |
| Trout: Rainbow (farmed) | Tilapia (Central America, farmed) | Tuna: Albacore, Bigeye, Yellowfin |
| Tuna: Albacore, incl. canned white | Tuna: Bigeye, Yellowfin (troll/pole) | (longline)* |
| tuna (troll/pole, U.S. and BC) | Tuna: Canned white/Albacore | Tuna: Bluefin* and Tongol |
| Tuna: Skipjack, including canned | (troll/pole except U.S. and BC) | Tuna: Canned (except troll/pole)* |
| light tuna (troll/pole) | | |

KEY   BC = British Columbia   CA = California   OR = Oregon   WA = Washington

\* = Limit consumption due to concerns about mercury or other contaminants

*Courtesy of Monterey Bay Aquarium*

land on our masts. Despite our rods being cast at every opportunity, we caught just three fish—a yellowfin and a skipjack tuna and a dorado—during our entire journey. So deprived were we of wildlife sightings that we were elated to come across giant, floating whale turds in the Tasman Sea. Turds! At least we had assurance whales were out there somewhere!

So where did all of that teeming sea life go in fifty-three years? It's quite possible that it's still out there and we were skunked due to the sound waves of *Plastiki*'s 12,500 bottles plowing through the ocean simply scaring away every fish and marine mammal for miles around. I doubt that. Dolphins and pilot whales have exquisitely fine-tuned hearing, and they didn't seem bothered.

I think the explanation for the lifeless sea was in part revealed to us one night between Christmas Island and Samoa. Jo was at the navigation desk and monitoring the location of three boats near us. Each was a longline fishing boat. She spoke over the radio to the captain of one boat who said he was trailing three thousand baited hooks. The boat was chasing bluefin tuna, a big, fast, beautifully streamlined swimmer that is critically endangered. Over the course of the night, the boat captain expected to pull in more than one hundred bluefin. In both the Pacific and Atlantic oceans, the bluefin is being hunted to extinction. And God help any other creature that catches hold of one of those three thousand hooks (like albatrosses—an estimated 100,000 are snagged on longline hooks each year). Their bodies will be mercilessly tossed overboard when the line is winched in.

By the standards of the long-lining industry, the boat we made contact with was a small fry. His three thousand hooks are dwarfed by industrial vessels that unspool trunk lines 60 miles long. Off of these, branch lines extend tens if not hundreds of feet in all directions. In all, some 500 miles of line can be deployed in one set, allowing a fishing vessel to gather 50 tons of fish in a single haul. These mammoth vessels remain at sea for months at a time, stashing their enormous catch in freezers below deck. Estimates of the number of long-line hooks set each year range up to then billion. Long-liners typically target one high-value fish, such as bluefin or swordfish, but of course that isn't all they catch. A report by the World Wildlife Fund of South Africa details how longline fishing off the west coast of South Africa,

EVERY TIME WE GO TO THE GROCERY OR A RESTAURANT, WE HOLD THE POWER TO PUT THE CLAMPS ON OVERFISHING.

Namibia, and Angola kills 33,850 seabirds, 4,200 sea turtles, and 7 million sharks every year. Factor that level of bycatch across the globe, and the amount of collateral and intentional death wrought by long-liners is truly staggering.

And yet compared to the killing efficiency of a modern factory supertrawler, the industrial long-liners seem almost sporting. Longer than a football field, trawlers can drag a purse seine that could swallow more than a dozen Boeing 747 aircraft. Floating slaughter centers, these trawlers are capable of catching and processing up to 200 tons of fish a day. In their wake, the ocean is swept clean. Words can only go so far in describing the carnage. I implore you to visit treehugger.com or YouTube.com and search for the footage from the BBC documentary *Fragile Paradise* in which two diver-filmmakers enter a purse seine net as it encircles a massive school of yellowfin tuna. More than 150 tons of tuna are caught in this slowly tightening trap. As the walls of netting constrict, the school panics. Fish jam their heads through the net holes and bloody themselves in an attempt to flee. Like the two divers interviewed afterward from the safety of

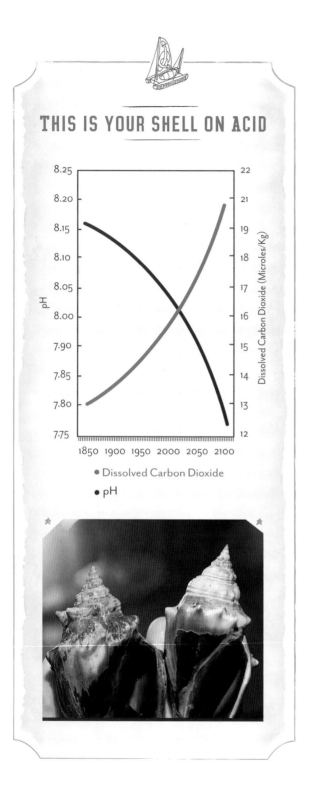

## THIS IS YOUR SHELL ON ACID

- Dissolved Carbon Dioxide
- pH

their skiff, like me after viewing it, you will be shaken by the sight of death on this scale.

Every time we go to the grocery or a restaurant, we hold the power to put the clamps on overfishing. Longline and factory trawler fishermen are merely responding to our desire for cheap, plentiful seafood. Buy only sustainably harvested or farmed seafood by downloading a pocket guide or smartphone app from the U.S.-centric Monterey Bay Aquarium's Seafood Watch (monterey bayaquarium.org) or the more internationally focused Marine Stewardship Council (msc.org).

To take further action, join the fight to remove government subsidies that prop up fishing fleets to the tune of $20 billion annually and thereby encourage fishermen to venture further and stay out longer than would be economically feasible otherwise. The non-profit group Oceana.org is working through the World Trade Organization to remove such subsidies. Poaching is another key contributor to overfishing. For example, the Chilean sea bass you last ate stands a 20 percent chance of having been pirated. The World Wildlife Fund, through its sustainable fishing program, leads an aggressive campaign to end poaching.

• • •

The oceans have taken a bullet for us. By absorbing one-third of the carbon dioxide humans have disgorged since the dawn of the Industrial Age through our burning of forests, coal, natural gas, and petroleum, the oceans have potentially slowed the process of global warming. Our current atmospheric $CO_2$ concentration is 392 parts per million, up from about 318 ppm fifty years ago, higher than it's been in at least 650,000 years and already long past the 350 ppm level many scientists feel is safe.

Yet without the oceans swallowing 525 billion tons of excess carbon each year, the level might be 435 ppm or more. And we'd be one giant step closer

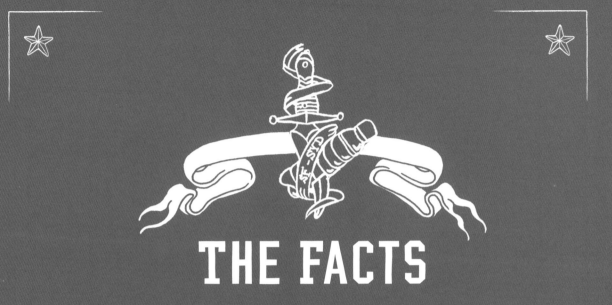

# THE FACTS

LESS THAN 1 PERCENT OF THE WORLD'S OCEANS
ARE PROTECTED FROM DESTRUCTIVE
FISHING PRACTICES.

THE DEMAND FOR SHARK-FIN SOUP
RESULTS IN THE KILLING OF AS MANY AS
73 MILLION SHARKS EACH YEAR.

AROUND THE WORLD, THOUSANDS OF SQUARE MILES OF CORAL HAVE BEEN "BLEACHED," OR HAVE DIED. SCIENTISTS BELIEVE WARMING SEA TEMPERATURES ARE TO BLAME—AND THAT THEY WILL CONTINUE TO RISE.

to climate mayhem. Our oceans are paying the cost of this generosity through rising acidification. For organisms that build shells or skeletons, like coral, mollusks, and other shellfish, and a whole range of free-floating, shell-forming creatures like coccoliths, pteropods, and foraminifera that form the base of the ocean food chain, acidifying seas are a deadly prospect. Given the fundamental role those creatures play in marine systems, if they're in trouble, then the oceans are in hot water.

In their natural state, the oceans are slightly alkaline. At the outset of the Industrial Age, ocean pH was 8.21. If you weren't dozing during high school chemistry class, you'll remember that a pH of 7 is neutral; anything above that (milk of magnesia, for instance, is 10) is alkaline, and anything below (tomato juice is 4) is considered acidic. Today, ocean pH has dropped to 8.1. During the next century, a business-as-usual approach to energizing our buildings and vehicles will accelerate acidification and result in an ocean pH of 7.824 by the year 2100.

Doesn't sound like much of a decline, does it? But the pH scale is logarithmic, meaning the slight 0.10 drop in pH to date represents a 30 percent increase in acidity. We have altered the basic chemistry of the oceans. The projected ocean pH of 7.824 would be lower than at any point in the past 20 million years! As $CO_2$ dissolves in ocean water, it binds with $H_2O$ molecules to form carbonic acid. I'll skip the complex chemical reaction that ensues and get to the result: less aragonite and calcite, two forms of calcium carbonate, in circulation. With less aragonite and calcite at their disposal, coral, mollusks, and other organisms will have difficulty building and maintaining their shells or skeletons. Think of it as osteoporosis for our little hard-bodied friends.

Already there is evidence that acidification is taking a toll on building-block species in the web of marine life. The weight of Antarctic foraminifera shells has declined 30 to 35 percent since the end of the eighteenth century. When French researchers subjected a type of free-

A VISIT BY A POD OF PILOT WHALES AS *PLASTIKI*
NEARED CHRISTMAS ISLAND WAS ONE OF ONLY
A HANDFUL OF ENCOUNTERS WITH WILDLIFE ON
THE EXPEDITION.

# CREW PROFILE: SINGELI AGNEW

Singeli was the pinch hitter who hit a clutch home run. When a replacement for Max, who took a hiatus at Christmas Island, fell through, Singeli was ready and able to fill in on short notice. She is a recognized photojournalist and documentary producer. She has lived and reported from India, Nepal, Cambodia and France, covering a wide range of social and scientific issues, including several stories for PBS Frontline/World, and her award-winning short documentary "Pollen Nation," the first film to look at the phenomena of industrialized pollination and migratory beekeeping.

### WERE YOU PREPARED FOR LIFE AT SEA?

I'm a landlubber, so I wasn't sure how I'd take to life at sea. I was onboard for less than a month though, so I think I got off easy; I didn't have to deal with the mental challenge of weeks upon weeks at sea as most of the crew did. My biggest issue was drinking enough water while we sailed through the tropics.

### FAVORITE PART OF THE DAY ON PLASTIKI?

I treasured being on watch at dawn. It was a quiet time on the boat, and always intensely beautiful to watch the night fade into day and catch the first glow of the sun on the waves.

### WHERE DID YOU RETREAT TO FOR A PRIVATE MOMENT?

I think the most private moments were simply being at the helm, when others were sleeping or keeping watch on another part of the boat. It required a lot of concentration to keep the course, and felt almost meditative at times because your mind would meld with the wind and the movement. I loved being so aware of the weather, and having the changing sky as a companion.

### A TREASURED MEMORY FROM THE JOURNEY?

Jo had a constellation book that described the night sky on each particular night, as well as the myths behind the constellations. I loved sitting with her in the middle of the night, reading with a headlamp and watching the drama revolving above our heads.

### BIGGEST WORK-RELATED CHALLENGE AT SEA?

I've never had to mix the logistics of living with the logistics of filming to such a degree. One moment I'd be washing dishes, and the next I'd be grabbing the camera to film an event. Also, it was a struggle to shoot on a cramped boat without getting the other camera mic in the shot. That drove me crazy.

### FIRST THING YOU DID ON DRY LAND?

Took a shower! Had a cold beer. Rejoiced in using my leg muscles again. Not necessarily in that order.

### YOUR LASTING IMPRESSION OF THE PACIFIC?

Before this trip, I thought of the Pacific as a monolithic body of water in-between continents. Now I feel it's a *place*, with so much happening.

floating mollusk at the base of the Arctic food chain to the ocean pH expected in 2100, their shells were 28

## CORAL REEFS ARE THE RAIN FORESTS OF THE OCEAN, AND LIKE THE RAIN FORESTS, WE'RE MOWING THEM DOWN.

percent thinner, and fewer than one-third of the tiny mollusks were active swimmers. The rest sank to the bottom of the test beaker. The effects of acidification on marine fauna are poorly understood and demand a lot more study. But is there time?

Ocean acidification might seem like an overwhelming problem—make no mistake, it won't be easy to reverse—but one person can make a difference. At the personal level, reduce your use of carbon-spewing fossil fuels by riding your bike and walking more, and driving a lot less. Cars are at their most inefficient when driven short distances. Invest in making your home as energy-efficient as possible. Your return in utility savings on every dollar invested in home energy–saving upgrades will exceed most anything available in the stock market. Walk the talk so you can encourage friends and family to think twice about their energy use. At the political level, get after your senators and congressional representatives to support a carbon tax that penalizes Planet 1.0 fuel sources like coal and oil and encourages innovation in Planet 2.0 renewable energies like solar, wind, tidal, and geothermal—and plain old conservation. Check out the Carbon Tax Center (www.carbontax.org) for more ways to advance this policy initiative.

• • •

Coral reefs are the rain forests of the ocean, and like the rain forests, we're mowing them down. Coral reefs cover just 1 percent of the earth's surface, but acre for acre they support a richer variety of life—more than 4,000 fish species—than any other marine environment. Around the globe they offer sanctuary and breeding ground for marine life, a buffer for shorelines against ocean waves, and sustenance for millions of people. They're also under tremendous assault.

Scientists estimate that we've killed off one-quarter of all coral reefs. In the Philippines, the loss is estimated at 70 percent, due to sediment runoff and destructive fishing practices. In the Seychelles and Maldives, 90 percent of the surrounding coral reefs were killed in the past few years, largely due to unusually high seawater temperatures.

For their tough exterior and the pounding they take from ocean waves, coral reefs are remarkably sensitive, especially to temperature change. They can tolerate only a very narrow range of ocean temperatures. Just one week of hotter- or colder-than-usual temperatures can kill coral. Warmer water will be a fact in a world beset by rising carbon dioxide levels. A 1.8 degrees Fahrenheit rise in ocean water temperature can cause serious bleaching of coral and eventual death. During 1997–98, the warmest year on record and a period of unusually high ocean temperatures, an estimated 16 percent of all coral reefs were severely damaged.

On its own, the warming of seawater would pose a grave threat to coral reefs. Combined with rising acidification of ocean water, which inhibits coral growth, as well as threats from fishing practices like dredging, methods for collecting tropical fish for aquariums like tossing dynamite into a reef to stun specimens, as well as sediment runoff from forest clearing, the margin for survival is tight and the outlook for reefs is dire. By at least one estimate, if the present rate of destruction continues, 70 percent of the world's coral reefs will be destroyed by the year 2050.

Every aquatic ecosystem is connected, so even

though you may live thousands of miles from a reef, the pesticides, fertilizers, drain cleaners, solvents, and other household products you use eventually will enter the ocean. Think twice about what you put down the drain, and use only safe, organic products to clean your home and care for your lawn and garden. Also, coral reefs need stakeholders, so visit a reef and snorkel or scuba dive with reef-friendly, local guides. Efforts to reduce your carbon footprint will help tame the big threats of bleaching and ocean acidification.

...

It's very clear to me that we can't keep going on with business as usual. The fantasy that the oceans will take what we dish out needs to end, if for no other reason than self-preservation. We are threatening our own life-support systems. In our actions toward the oceans, I'm reminded of the game Jenga, in which players carefully extract wooden blocks from a rickety tower they've built. We're pulling out species and vital components from the marine environment without a thought to the systemic effect. At some point, perhaps sooner rather than later, we could pull the wrong block and invite biological collapse.

We are up against it. In soccer terms—my favorite sport—we're down by two goals with less than five minutes on the clock. In our favor is the ocean's amazing ability to regenerate. I may be a blind optimist, but I think people will react before that biological breakdown happens. There are hopeful signs of changing attitudes and fantastic programs like the Sylvia Earle Foundation's Mission Blue (see page 108), which has pinpointed the last pristine environments in our ocean for preservation, and Conservation International's brilliant viral campaign to get people to save a square mile of ocean.

With leadership, with awareness, and with the ability to allow our oceans the chance to breathe by stopping our exploitation, I think we can create a sea change.

## HOPE FOR THE OCEANS

The problems besetting the oceans are immense, and time is running out, but we can reverse the damage and restore ocean vitality. The key will be safeguarding hot spots of biological diversity, or "Hope Spots," as Sylvia Earle's foundation, Mission Blue, calls them. Still relatively unscathed by pollution, overfishing, and other human assault, these eighteen Hope Spots must be locked away as marine-protected areas to save critical habitats and preserve biodiversity. It's an opportunity we cannot lose.

CORAL SEA: One of the last intact tropical oceanic ecosystems and home to whales, sharks, turtles, and a healthy population of big fish, Australia's Coral Sea is just 1 percent protected.

CHILEAN FJORDS AND ISLANDS: Home to seals, whales, dolphins, and other marine mammals, the southern fjords, Juan Fernández Islands, and Easter Island are threatened by overfishing and the strip-mining effect of bottom trawlers.

GULF OF GUINEA: Uninhabited beach and unspoiled waters are imperiled by oil drilling, poaching of leatherback turtle eggs, and industrial fishing.

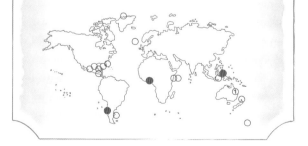

## THERE IS NO BOX

### BY LOUIE PSIHOYOS

About five years ago, after having just founded the Oceanic Preservation Society, a nonprofit for which I am the executive director, my family and I were invited to spend some time on a friend's boat in the Caribbean. Next to us was a charter boat, and on it, Steven Spielberg and his family. At fifty years old, I had not quite worked out the details of my first significant career change—for two decades I had been a photographer for *National Geographic, Time, Sports Illustrated,* and other major magazines, but I was preparing to make documentaries that would bring attention to and hopefully inspire people to save our oceans. I had never attempted a film before.

At some point, Steven came over for a visit. My son was about the same age as one of his sons, and they had become easy friends, even doing sleepovers on the boats as if jumping from trailer to trailer in a mobile home park. In the course of conversation, he asked what I did for a living. With only a slight hesitation and a modest amount of irony, I asked the great director, who was in the middle of making *War of the Worlds,* what advice he had for a first-time filmmaker.

He thought about if for a second and said, "Never make a movie involving boats or animals."

I laughed uncomfortably.

A few months later, I discovered a forbidden place in a national park in Japan that would come to be known simply as "the cove." More dolphins are killed here than any other place in the world; it is guarded by dogs, motion sensors, police, and a series of tunnels, high fences with spikes, and barbed wire. If we were to be caught in the chaos of traps and obstacles that surround the cove, attempting to make the goings on there known to the world, we would have faced arrest and possibly great bodily harm by the people who have a vested interest in protecting the cove's great secret. The people of Taiji, Japan, who kill these dolphins have little respect for life and were known to become violent at the sight of Westerners in their town. Despite the obvious reasons not to, I knew I would make my first movie on the cove—complete with boats, animals, and deliberate trespassing, facing foreign arrest, and subjects who would rather kill us than speak to our cameras. We were thinking outside the box, as it were.

Needless to say, I wasn't about to call up Mr. Spielberg and ask if he approved of my career path. But our documentary, *The Cove*, which *Rolling Stone* called "A cross between *Flipper* and *The Bourne Identity*," went on to win at Sundance, the Academy Awards, and about seventy-five awards in between, including the Peter Benchley Award. (Benchley wrote *Jaws*, which would later put Spielberg on the map.)

*The Cove* would not go on to make boatloads of money like *Jaws*, but our little movie helped save the lives of dolphins in Japan and ignited an awareness about the stress they face in captivity—the likes of which the animal rights community has been trying to foster for decades. The documentary also contributed to policies that would change how these animals are treated in domestic dolphin "abusement" parks. To me, those acts, generated as a result of having seen *The Cove*, are the truest measure of our film's success, not a $10 ticket and a box of popcorn. Anyone who lives, works, or plays on the ocean knows that we are losing this environment at a staggering pace, in a real life war being played out in real time. *The Cove* was just one assault of many that will be needed to galvanize a critical mass of support for our oceans. And I believe documentaries are weapons of mass construction—drop a bomb and you kill people; make a movie and you advance the collective consciousness. You create allies.

Filmmaking has become my outlet for ocean advocacy. In that way it's my *Plastiki*, my long voyage. I would encourage each and every person to find your own individual expression, your own *Plastiki*. Use your talents—as a lawyer, businessperson, artist, or voting citizen—to fight for the world's oceans now. And do it your way, because there are no rules when it comes to saving the planet. There is no box around an open heart.

. . .

*Louie Psihoyos is a photographer and filmmaker. His 2009 film,* The Cove, *won an Academy Award for documentary feature.*

**9**

NEXT STOP, OZ

ON THE FINAL LEG OF *PLASTIKI*'S JOURNEY, THE CREW FIGHTS ITS HIGHEST WINDS AND SEAS, A ROGUE TANKER, AND A MEDIA FIRESTORM—AND FACES THE BITTERSWEET END OF THE VOYAGE.

ON ANY EXPEDITION, THERE'S A FINE LINE BETWEEN BEING
DOGGED AND BEING RECKLESS. FIXATING ON A GOAL SKEWS JUDGMENT.
AND THAT CAN GET PEOPLE KILLED.

Peel back most any headline-grabbing disaster on high mountains, polar ice, open ocean, or anywhere else that men and women challenge themselves in extreme environments where the margin for error is slim, and you'll find a tipping point where things started to unravel but the warning signs either were ignored or overridden. Mountaineers call such blinding desire "summit fever."

Sober risk assessment isn't easily done when there is so much invested time and money and momentum behind an expedition. But knowing when to push on and when to turn around is crucial in leading safe adventures. So it was in Samoa that I wrestled with the decision to cut our adventure short.

As we sailed Polynesia, Jo, Mr. T, and the rest of the crew had noticed greater than usual movement in *Plastiki*'s structure. We expected some degree of flexing—the boat was designed to give with the waves and wind—but not too much. On close inspection in a boatyard in Apia, the capital of Samoa, we discovered the cause: buckling in six of the thirty-two brackets that

reinforced the connections between deck beams and the twin hulls. These boomerang-shape brackets—four on each of eight beams—acted as shock absorbers allowing the hulls some movement. Like forensic detectives at a crime scene, we tried to pinpoint the cause of damage. Our prime suspect: the rigging leading to the mainmast.

A sailboat's mast gains stability from wire shrouds and stays strung from the top down to attachment points on the outside edge of the deck. As the wind pushes against the sail, it loads, or tensions, the rigging on the windward side while slightly slackening the leeward rigging. On *Plastiki*, that tugging of the shrouds and stays, in combination with intense tropical heat that had softened the Seretex material the brackets were made of, caused the rigging to loosen. Being good sailors, we'd dutifully ratcheted the turnbuckles at the base of each shroud and stay to keep things nice and tight. We didn't know it, but we were gradually pulling our boat apart. Like a cartoon car whose wheels splay when one too many elephants

AFTER NEARLY 8,000 MILES OF OPEN SEA, *PLASTIKI* EXHIBITED SIGNS OF ITS MONTHS OF HARD USE AND EXPOSURE. BUT SHE STILL SAILED TRUE.

DAVID, MATT, AND MR. T TOOK THE OPPORTUNITY
TO GET TRADITIONAL SAMOAN TATTOOS.

piles aboard, *Plastiki*'s twin hulls were flared apart a little at the keels.

That knowledge left me with a pressing question: Was *Plastiki* beyond repair? And if not, how sure could I be that she wouldn't fail later in a way that put the crew at risk mid-ocean?

To get the answers, we flew the boat's designer, Andy Dovell, to Samoa from his home base in Australia. Those few days awaiting Andy's arrival were anxious times. Jo, Mr. T, and the Samoan shipwrights we hired were confident the damage wasn't serious, yet it was entirely possible Andy might get in under the craft and decide otherwise and condemn our boat.

Did I want to reach Sydney? Absolutely. But the *Plastiki* project was always bigger than the actual adventure. Its ultimate success did not hinge on making it to Australia. The boat was a metaphor for solutions and change in the way we deal with disposable plastics, a traveling basket of inquisitiveness put into action. In my mind, the fact that we had built an iconic boat in strict adherence to cradle-to-cradle principles and sailed it from San Francisco to Christmas Island across one of the largest open stretches of water on our planet, arriving with boat and crew in good shape, was triumph enough.

The media and blogosphere saw it differently. For them, it was Sydney or bust, and anything less would brand us failures. These were the same wags who insisted *Plastiki* wouldn't make it out of San Francisco Bay, or wouldn't sail clear of U.S. waters, or wouldn't survive in the open Pacific. With every gain we made, they shifted the goal posts. I learned a long time ago that there are some people you just can't please. Hell, we could make it to Sydney and the skeptics would wonder why we fell short of Perth.

While waiting for Andy, we made productive use of the downtime working out Jo's solution for preventing further damage to the twenty-six structural brackets that were still intact. We would swap out *Plastiki*'s stainless steel rigging for rope. "The rope acts as a shock absorber to the loads being generated as a result of the pressures caused through the sails and motion of us riding the waves," Jo explained. "Reducing these point loads in turn reduces the pressure going through the beams." On a sailboat, however, you don't reduce forces on one part of the craft without transferring them somewhere else. Exactly where those forces would go would come as a rude surprise in the weeks ahead.

Apia, with boatyard facilities and talented craftsmen, was a godsend for our limping vessel. Jo and Singeli seemed particularly taken with every idea put forth by Trevor, a very handsome, tousle-haired local marine engineer. "A right fittie," Jo chirped. We commissioned a woodworker to build a leeboard to improve the steering of the boat. The final product—an eight-foot-long, three-foot-wide foil-shaped wing, stained and shellacked—was almost too pretty to sink out of sight. We would be able to insert it through an improvised holster on the leeward side of the boat to prevent our sideways crabbing, thus allowing us to cut closer to the wind. We needed every advantage to make Sydney.

WHILE PLASTIKI WAS IN THE SHOP, A FEW OF THE CREW, ME AMONG THEM, RECEIVED PERMANENT AND VERY PERSONAL REMINDERS OF OUR TIME IN THESE PARADISIAL ISLANDS.

While *Plastiki* was in the shop, a few of the crew, me among them, received permanent and very personal reminders of our time in these paradisial islands. Samoan tattoos are known for their size, covering whole swaths of skin in intricate patterns resembling shirts or shorts, and, at least in old times, for the painful process

PREPARATIONS TO LEAVE SAMOA WERE
EXTENSIVE INCLUDING REPAIR TO *PLASTIKI*'S
DAMAGED STRUCTURAL SUPPORTS.

## PRIZE-WINNING WAYS TO BEAT WASTE

Nobody is as smart as everybody. That's the credo behind Adventure Ecology's work. Human ingenuity can solve the big environmental problems besetting us—such as plastics in the marine environment—and lead us toward a sustainable economy that's in tune with natural systems. Which is why in the summer of 2010, Adventure Ecology partnered with Myoo Create, a new crowd-sourcing platform, to launch the Beat Waste Start-Up Challenge, an open competition with a $25,000 prize awarded to new businesses with innovative and scalable solutions that will make the dream of a zero-waste future a reality. The number and quality of the submissions were inspirational. Here are some of the winners:

**Eco-Artrepreneurship Programme.** Young Filipino artists work with unemployed mothers to make and sell a line of biodegradable household cleaners and detergents, as well as curtains, bags, and papers made from recycled materials.

**Rentalic.** Need a tent for a weekend camping trip but don't want to purchase a new one? Through person-to-person renting, Rentalic matches people who need stuff with people who have stuff to reduce overconsumption.

**Pick Up America.** Four recent college grads on an eighteen-month walking tour across America are organizing trash cleanups with school, church, and community groups. The group is also trying to inspire a transition to a zero-waste society by getting people to think twice about buying and using disposable items.

used to mark the skin. I commissioned three tattoos: on my left foot, X marks the spot; five arrows on my right foot, each representing a member of my family; and on my elbow, three lines, representing the North Pole, the South Pole, and a dotted line for the equator. The top line's shark-tooth detail is a Samoan symbol for unity. Matt and Mr. T joined me under the tattoo gun.

When Andy Dovell arrived in Apia, I emphasized to him that I wanted to be overly conservative in our decision making. Safety of the crew was paramount. His assessment of *Plastiki*'s condition brought the best possible news. With some modifications, our boat was still seaworthy. He recommended reinforcing the compromised boomerang brackets with aluminum struts to correct the splaying of the hulls and to prevent future

ON JUNE 13, AFTER A MUCH LONGER STOPOVER IN SAMOA THAN ANY OF US WOULD HAVE LIKED, PLASTIKI SET SAIL AGAIN ON WHAT PROMISED TO BE THE TOUGHEST LEG OF THE JOURNEY SO FAR.

buckling. Naturally, we would have preferred carrying out this minor design adjustment using Seretex, but we were up against the clock. The nearest Seretex was many miles away. The longer we waited, the stronger the winter storms roaring through the Tasman Sea would be.

On June 13, after a much longer stopover in Samoa than any of us would have liked, *Plastiki* set sail again on what promised to be the toughest leg of the journey so far. Our boat was shipshape, but were we home free? Hardly. I couldn't guarantee we'd make it to Australia. We stood a very good chance of making it as far as New Caledonia only to be thwarted from crossing the Tasman by violent storms.

AT TOP, PHOTOGRAPHER LUCA BABINI TAKES CARE OF GRAHAM HILL'S HAIR; ABOVE, LUCA AND DAVID MARK THEIR LONG JOURNEY TOGETHER.

THE FINAL DAYS OF THE TRIP OFFERED SOME
MOMENTS OF PEACE AND REFLECTION
ON THE MEANING OF *PLASTIKI*.

But the weather that day was perfect, the boat handled better than ever, and we were enjoying a reunion of sorts. Max and Vern, our compadres from the first leg of the journey, were back, replacing Luca and Singeli, who had departed for home. Matt Grey, *Plastiki*'s expedition manager, was joining us for the last leg, which was only appropriate. Matt had worked on the *Plastiki* project longer than anyone yet had never sailed the boat on blue water. I was excited for him and for us. Matt is a restless tinkerer, good strategist, and fine company. With Graham remaining aboard, we were at full and rollicking capacity with a crew of seven.

## CREW VIEW: VERN MOEN

Coming back to the boat, there's a certain nostalgia with *Plastiki*. I noticed it for the first time when I lay down in my bed—the same one: top bunk, port side. It was always a game to keep from falling off with the rocking of the boat. There are about four or five positions that I discovered on that first leg, and I found myself naturally settling into one of those identical positions. Even sitting at the "living room" table, with dozens of stored-away, swinging limes hitting me in the head, brings back memories.

Two days in, I'm already enjoying it much more than the first leg. The weather is warm and squally, so we get more rain, which is invaluable when you're constantly sweating and traveling too quickly to swim. Waking up for shifts has been easier. I still wouldn't say it's enjoyable, but when you have warm weather and a steady breeze outside, life is just a bit brighter than when you're woken up by the other shift and they're in full weather gear, shivering and dripping water all over the cabin. That's the opposite of enjoyable.

.........................

Our course southwest from Samoa would take us through the heart of Melanesia. Beachgoers know it as a nirvana of gorgeous, palm-fringed islands surrounded by some of the purest ocean in the world. For a vessel that sails at the whim of winds and currents, Melanesia is a minefield. Jo and Mr. T would have to be incredibly careful not to ground us as we navigated treacherous shoals, shallows, and low-lying atolls that are visible only when you're practically upon them. Around-the-world racers like our two skippers typically stick to the southern oceans below the 40th parallel, where the winds howl and deep water rules. Sailing *Plastiki* through Polynesia was like a vacation for Jo and Mr. T, yet stressful in a way very different from helming a multimillion-dollar speed machine on which the slightest movement of the tiller can win or lose your race.

A truism aboard *Plastiki* was the higher the sailing speed, the better everyone's spirits. There's something about smashing through waves and leaving a foaming wake—real sailing, damn it!—that feels right and uplifting. The crossing from Samoa around the northernmost atoll of the Fiji Islands featured some of our briskest sailing yet. We covered serious mileage, and everyone was on a high. Over a nearly two-week span, we averaged 5.5 knots per hour and even kicked it up to 8 knots for an entire memorable day. "Awesome" was the general consensus.

But which way would we go from there? Rounding Fiji to the north and sailing for Noumea at the southeast corner of New Caledonia presented the most direct route to Coffs Harbor on Australia's Gold Coast, our intended goal from the outset. Also, Noumea, the capital of New Caledonia, offered a safe harbor to wait out weather systems until a window opened for us to sprint for Australia. On the downside, steering for Noumea meant holding a tighter angle into the prevailing southerly wind—never an easy task on *Plastiki*—and exposing boat and crew to a belt of stronger trade winds, currently blowing at 35 knots, and associated rough seas.

A SUDDEN STORM ON THE TASMAN SEA HAD THE
MOST DANGEROUS WAVES OF THE VOYAGE, MADE
WORSE BY A TORN SAIL THE CREW HAD TO REPAIR.

Alternatively, navigating to the north of New Caledonia, while minimizing the risk of getting caught in strong headwinds and big swells, required dodging islands and reefs in the Vanuatu Islands and even greater navigational challenges in the shallow Coral Sea. If a big storm rolled up the coast of Australia, we'd have no port of refuge on this course. And, ultimately, that course would lead to landfall on Australia near Bundaberg, a good 500 miles off the mark from Sydney.

To complicate matters, we made an unnerving discovery: our mainmast and mizzenmast were wobbling in their bases. Uh-oh. Remember us changing our rigging from wire to rope in Samoa? That retrofit changed the flex of our boat. Whereas previously everything moved in unison so that the loads of the rigs carried throughout the whole superstructure, now the central sections of the hulls, in between the inboard main crossbeams, were stiff, while the bow and stern sections still flexed. We could tension the shrouds running from the mast down to the port and starboard sides of the boat, but it was impossible to gain tension on the fore and aft stays.

Hence the teetering masts and, believe it or not, ripping sails. Since embarking from Samoa, our headsails (aka jibs), the big sails that unfurl from the forestays at the bows of the twin hulls, were blowing apart at the seams with frustrating regularity. When that happened, it necessitated frantic team efforts to yank down the ripped sail and replace it with either another headsail or a smaller storm jib. Invariably, the headsails would rip in the dead of night when swells were crashing over the bow. Going forward in the dark on one of the narrow bows to deal with a ruptured sail required the agility of a gymnast and the balance of a rodeo rider. As you clutched the faulty sail between your knees and painstakingly threaded the new one into place, the bow would buck up and down and waves would surely pummel you. Once the damaged sail was retrieved, it then fell to Jo, Mr. T, or Max, our designated seamstresses, to stitch the torn sail back together. I couldn't figure out the relationship between the wobbling mainmast and the ripping headsails until Jo explained it. "Since the bows are flexible, as we come up a big wave the head stays relaxed. Then they tension again as we sail down the wave, adding a snatch load to the headsail and blowing it out," she said.

When the wind and waves eased a bit, Mr. T was able to hoist himself to the top of the mainmast to rig a few extra stabilizing runners. That did the trick, limiting movement in the mainmast. We received assurance via satellite phone from Andy Dovell and Buzz Ballenger, the mast designer, that slight movement, while not ideal, wasn't too serious. We would just have to be extra careful with the winds and swells we took on during the last days of our journey.

In Jo's ongoing chess match with the weather—a complicated algorithm going on in her head involving wind direction and speed, current, *Plastiki*'s sideways crabbing, and the short-range and long-term weather forecast—her opponent flinched. A forecast of favorable winds and lower wave height allowed us to break for Noumea. We set a course between Fiji and Vanuatu for the southern tip of New Caledonia. In the interests of making as much southerly progress as possible, we would sacrifice speed and even sail backward a bit toward the east. As if she didn't have enough to consider, one more factor entered Jo's calculations during this run: the wooden leeboard custom-built in Samoa suddenly lost its bite. How was that possible? We pulled it out of its holster and at first it looked like a shark had snapped our leeboard in half. It turned out to be the force of the ocean, just as fearsome.

## CREW VIEW: MATT GREY

Only a few days or nights ago we were still helming in just shorts on a dry deck beneath a cascading moon.

Flying fish were dancing in our shadows, sometimes vaulting onto the deck and glistening in the moonlight. Now I stagger out into the rain, wet trousers clinging to my skin and my warm tea clutched to my chest.

Welcome to winter in the Southern Hemisphere. Another rough night heralds another dawn, and we breathe a secret sigh of relief. The perilous nature of our situation is rarely discussed, but I feel it each time a mighty wave cracks the boat. I search for sounds in the night, clues to the abnormal, and I know the others do too. I must say, I admire the stoicism on board; it seems to be born out of a refreshing mix of fearlessness, mania, and fated resolve. We are here. It's where we're at. It's what we've got.

...........................

The night felt like it was hiding a surprise. The air was heavy and oppressive, the sea perfectly flat. And it was dark. So dark I couldn't see the hand in front of my face. Lightning punched through the cloud deck, matched in the inky water below by pulses of phosphorescence. Mr. T, Vern, and I were on "dog watch," the 1:00 to 4:00 A.M. shift. Noumea was several days behind us, a pleasant port call where we waited out several storms and Max, our Frenchman, went positively bonkers on New Caledonia's French-influenced culture. At the risk of stereotype, he brought aboard armfuls of crisp baguettes and bags of haricots verts, and got to work preparing Michelin-worthy repasts, all the while whistling "La Marseillaise." We were minus Graham, a victim of the siren call of work and life demands back home in New York City. We had him for 11 weeks, and already I missed his cheerful presence and wry humor.

I was just finished with my hour at the helm, a slot of time devoted to pulling and flicking the tiller in a vain attempt to keep our becalmed boat on course. I'd retreated to the cabin to play a game of chess on the iPhone when I had this odd impulse to go outside and

# CREW PROFILE: LUCA BABINI

Throughout the building of *Plastiki*, every small triumph, wrenching failure, and major milestone was marked by one constant: Luca snapping away with his camera. As *Plastiki*'s official photographer, Luca was there from the outset. He is an internationally renown fashion photographer whose work has appeared in *Vogue*, *Glamour*, and *Esquire*, and hung on the wall of numerous galleries in Europe and the U.S. Of late, his work has concentrated on the issues of plastics in the ocean and international refugees.

### WERE YOU MENTALLY AND PHYSICALLY PREPARED FOR LIFE AT SEA?

No, I had forgotten all about it and to be able to free more than a month to be on *Plastiki*, I had to work 24/7 until the last minute. When I got on board *Plastiki*, I was exhausted.

### CRAZIEST THING THAT HAPPENED ON BOARD?

Being doused with liquid garbage after crossing the Equator.

### FAVORITE PART OF THE DAY ON PLASTIKI?

The night.

### FAVORITE SEA CREATURES?

Seahorse and lobster.

### WHAT DID YOU IMAGINE YOUR MUST HAVE ITEM ONBOARD WOULD BE?

An inflatable pool.

### WHERE DID YOU RETREAT TO FOR A MOMENT OF PRIVACY ONBOARD?

Inside the inflatable tender, which doubled up as my bed on most nights.

### BIGGEST CHALLENGE AT SEA?

Washing dishes in the dark on deck under heavy seas.

### FIRST THING YOU DID ON DRY LAND?

I kissed it.

### YOUR LASTING IMPRESSION OF THE PACIFIC?

The ocean is very ill. We need to act fast.

### WHAT WAS THE MOST ANTICIPATED PART OF YOUR JOURNEY?

Falling asleep with the universe as a blanket.

# INSPIRED BY PLASTIKI

Although only six or seven people crewed *Plastiki* at a time, thousands more sailed along with us in spirit through *Plastiki*'s website, which challenged viewers to take the *Plastiki* Pledge to reduce personal use of plastic; through social networking sites like Facebook and Twitter; and through the many news articles and TV shows that tracked our progress toward Sydney. In ways big and small, *Plastiki*'s message that together we can beat waste inspired change in many people or, as Robyn Lockwood, a kindergarten teacher in Australia, said, "The small drop has bigger ripples."

"I have fulfilled my pledge. I have stopped using plastic water bottles and have switched to a multi-use bottle instead. Totally."

— VALERIE PIRES

"I bought two *Plastiki* Klean Kanteens for home and work to drastically reduce my use of plastic bottles. I just have to find a way to reduce when I go out to eat. Where there is a will…."

— CHRISTINE C. COSTA

"Our family will be following your adventure and talking about it to our friends and community. Thanks for stepping out of comfort to bring awareness to the world."

— TONIE R. DEL CASTILLO

"My children (ages ten and five) and I spend our summer collecting plastic containers left behind by people and washed onto the beach. We should all contribute to cleaning the planet!"

— ALICE GRILLO

"My wife and I are avid boaters, and we are always stopping the boat to pick up trash in the water. I hope that this journey brings the much-needed attention that plastic garbage deserves. Keep up the good work!"

— TIM SICKEL

"I am age nine. Your adventure inspired me to create a chandelier made of plastic bottle caps for my class's experiments and creations project. It is amazing. My school would like to invite you and your crew to come in and talk to us about plastic and your trip. Remember that we are the future and that we love Mother Earth."

— SAMMIE OSBORN

"I am the kindergarten teacher at St. Francis Xavier Primary School in Woolgoolga, Australia. As part of our teaching unit on water, we are dispensing information about the *Plastiki* expedition throughout the whole school of some 200 children and as an update to all their parents. Our principal is an avid no-plastics campaigner with one day a week being a 'nude food' day, meaning no disposable plastics at all."

— ROBYN LOCKWOOD

"I work in a project at Grand-Popo, Benin. We care about environmental themes at the coast, and our biggest problem there is plastic. After we heard from the *Plastiki,* we had the idea to build another boat that uses plastic bottles to float. Our boat could be smaller and only for short trips near the Atlantic Coast, but it would be very interesting for my partners in Africa and for me."

— FABIAN STETTENBENZ

"We are Brita water-filter addicts ever since seeing the images of the Pacific garbage vortex."

— ANIKO M. E. BOEHLER

"My border collie, Sophie, and I walk along the beach at Ferry Point along San Francisco Bay pretty much every day. We collect all the plastic we can off the beaches."

— DEB CASTELLANA

"Your work highlighting the impact of plastic pollution first caught our attention on Oprah's Earth Day special in 2009. Actually seeing the devastation in the oceans and on marine life inspired us to invent the Veggie Bed reusable produce bag system, which can replace more than 1,000 plastic produce bags in its useful life."

— ANDREA STARN VINCENT

"Just wanted to show you how the *Plastiki* had inspired my five-year-old son's recycle project for school. We have been really interested in the mission. I thought this would be an exciting project to be taken into schools."

— LORNA

"Serving only tap water at my office in Hamburg, Germany. Good way to raise awareness and...it's tasty. Plus, clients like the idea behind it."

— GIANNA POSSEHL

"I will be picking up plastic bottles on South Padre Island in Texas. The Gulf of Mexico currents drop off a lot of plastics, and the locals don't help when it comes to keeping the dunes clean. We need much more awareness in this part of the world."

— BETINHA EMMERT SCHULTZ

"I set up a date to have students at my school go on a field trip to several parks and volunteer to clean up and plant new trees!"

— RICA BEJARIN

"I am ten years old. I was very upset last year to learn about the garbage dump in our oceans. Thank you for doing so much for our future! I plan on becoming an environmentalist/marine biologist when I grow up so I can find a way to clean up the oceans for the marine life."

— JACKIE WILLIAMS

check for other boats. I'd never felt that urge before, and I could count on one hand the number of other boats we'd seen. But sure enough, as I peeked around the corner of the cabin toward the bow, I could see the glow of a ship.

"Hey, Mr. T, there is a fairly large boat just off our port side."

"I know. Vern mentioned it. How close?"

"Close enough."

"Take the tiller."

Mr. T disappeared inside the cabin and returned with a pair of binoculars. "Can't see any navigation lights right now. Oh, hang on. I can see his port light. I'm going to try and call him."

"Hey, Mr. T? Mr. T! I am pretty sure I can see port and starboard lights. This guy's coming straight for us."

"Vern—take the man-overboard spotlight and shine it on the sails. David—try and keep to the starboard side of him. I'm going to try and get him on the radio again!"

"Vern, this guy is coming at us. Mr. T, he's getting close."

"I know, David. Be quiet. I'm trying to get hold of him. F***! He's not answering. Vern, shine that torch on the sail. Now!"

"I am, but this light is shit! It's already running out of juice. Great."

"This boat is going to ram us! Mr. T, we need to do something and fast."

"I know, David. Please be quiet! I'm trying to get him on the radio."

Adrenaline rushed through my veins. My arms and legs shook. Can't this guy see us? So why is he heading straight for us? We're in the middle of nowhere, and this ship decides on a path that's got us right in the crosshairs.

"Mr. T, we better do something right now or we're going to collide! He's closing fast! Really fast!"

"David, please! I am trying! He's just not answering! I can't seem to get him on the AIS [automatic identification system]. Just steer around him."

"Steer around him? Our boat's not even moving! Wait, he's turning! He must have seen us! He's turning! Yee-ha! Thank god for that! *Plastiki* lives another day!"

My body went limp with relief. We watched in awe as a big, black wall of steel slid silently past within what felt like spitting distance. *Forest Harmony* was the name written across the stern.

Mr. T quickly lit up a cigarette. "Phew! That was a really close call. You know it's close when you can smell the diesel. Can you go wake the other watch?"

It seemed I had barely tucked in at the end of our watch and sunk into the deepest possible slumber than I was being jerked into consciousness. Why is someone yelling at me?

"All hands on deck. Now! Quick, get up!" barked Mr. T.

"Wh-what's going on?"

"We're heaving to. Major wind shift."

"Hoven who?"

"Just get your gear on fast and make sure you're clipped on."

Bang! A huge wave slammed the cabin. Then another. My adrenaline, only recently subsided from the near collision, shot right back up into the red zone. Outside, all was chaos. Fearsome wind gusts slammed the boat and crew. Cresting waves 15 feet high were surging past, their tops blown flat and trailing horsetails of white spray. Everything was white and frothing, like

IN THE FINAL DAYS OF SAILING, THE CREW WAS EAGER TO REACH LAND BUT STILL ENJOYED THE NOW WELL-KNOWN ROUTINES OF *PLASTIKI*.

a mid-ocean blizzard. The mainsail and headsail were pinned very obviously on the wrong side of the boat, and the mast was leaning at a crazy angle. My first thought was: Are we going to capsize?

I would learn later that the wind, which had been coming gently out of the west-southwest, swung without warning to the south-southeast and came at *Plastiki* at 71 miles per hour, just 4 mph shy of hurricane force. The sudden wind shift flung the mainsail and headsail to the opposite side of the boat, catching Jo, Matt, and Max off guard. In a normal sailboat, the skipper would resolve the crisis by bringing the boat around to point directly into the wind, allowing the crew to drop sails and ride out the tempest. Not so *Plastiki*. Taking the wind full on, the sails wouldn't drop. We had to get the sails down before our already wobbly mast snapped or toppled, and the only way to do that was to physically grab the sailcloth in our hands and pull it down.

"Matt, take the helm," yelled Jo. "Vern, Mr. T, DR, and Max—up front with me."

A wall of seawater crashed down on us as we inched toward the bow. With each blow, I grabbed for the cabin or rigging and hung on for dear life, my arms pulled nearly out of their sockets. To my left, Max and Vern looked spooked. Nice to see I wasn't alone in that sentiment.

"I'm not sure I have the qualifications for this," shouted Vern with a grin.

"You mean survival?" I yelled back.

"Mr. T! Mr. T! Where the hell is Mr. T?" Jo screamed. I'd never heard her raise her voice like this before.

From under the headsail, Mr. T's head came tunneling up like a badger leaving its hole. Bang! Another mass of water smashed onto the hulls and us, salt spray pushing up under my eyelids. Please don't flip us. Thud! Another huge body blow to the underside of *Plastiki*.

"Holy shit, the mast is almost 90 degrees," I yelled.

"Incoming!" gasped Max.

Between waves, the five of us grabbed and pulled down the headsail. "Like hanging onto the cape of a flying grizzly bear," Vern described it later.

"Vern, take the sail and head back to the cockpit now," shouted Jo. "You too, Mr. T. David, help me reef the mainsail."

Reefing—lowering the sail partway and lashing the spare sailcloth—maintains control over direction of travel while keeping something really bad from happening—a wrecked mainsail, snapped mast, or capsizing being among the choicer options. Since the mainsail wasn't coming down on its own and I enjoy a one-foot height advantage over Jo, it was up to me to monkey up the mast, insert a finger into the grommet at the reef point four feet up the sail, and pull down.

"Can you grab it?"

"I'm trying! It just keeps slipping. There's too much pressure in the sail."

"Ease the main!" Jo yelled to Max. With that, she put her shoulder under my bum and pushed me up.

"Grab this and clip it in!" she said, handing me a carabiner.

"Got it." With my full weight hanging off the sail, I was finally able to bring it down.

"Great. Let's get back to the helm. Stay low."

"Whose watch is it?"

"It's you, Matt, and Mr. T."

Just another day at the office.

### CREW VIEW: VERN MOEN

Not every wave crashes on the side of *Plastiki*. Ninety percent just pick the boat up and, after passing under, drop us into the trough. At the bottom of the trough, you look up the wave face, and it might as well be 100 feet of water. Your stomach sinks as you wonder if this will be the one that crashes on your crying little face. I've tried filming these waves, trying to put them

# ELEVEN THINGS YOU CAN DO TO SAVE THE OCEANS

SEAL YOUR HOUSE. Lower the thermostat, save a mollusk. Heating and cooling the home accounts for your largest contribution of $CO_2$ into the atmosphere, which drives ocean acidification. Take steps to cut energy use by caulking cracks and adding insulation, and you'll save money, too.

DRIVE LESS; WALK MORE. Your car poses a threat to ocean health, due to the $CO_2$ it emits and the amount of oil spilled during drilling and shipping the oil to power it. Bike or walk on errands around town and use public transportation as much as possible.

USE LESS WATER. Every gallon of water used around the house is pulled from a natural ecosystem (a big concern in arid regions) and must be purified and pumped. Cut your flow by installing water-saving showerheads and aerators on faucets, and run the washing machine only with a full load.

CHOOSE SEAFOOD CAREFULLY. Entire species of fish are being hunted to extinction. Or, in the case of wild shrimp, the damage done in their pursuit is too costly. (Drag nets essentially strip-mine the ocean floor.) Download a handy smartphone app from montereybayaquarium.org that points the way to sustainable fish.

DUMP THE DRUGS SAFELY. Unused or expired pharmaceuticals flushed down the toilet contribute to the growing problem of drugs accumulating in aquatic ecosystems and showing up in drinking water. Dispose of old or unused drugs safely by grinding up pills, mixing them with used coffee grounds or kitty litter, and stashing them in a sealable yogurt tub before throwing them away.

VISIT A CAR WASH. Washing your car at home saves money, but all that soap goes right down the storm drain. Commercial car washes are required to clean and reuse waste water.

RUB OUT SKIN SCRUB. Exfoliating soaps, body washes, and skin scrubs get their grit from tiny plastic particles that go down the drain and then get into the food chain. Check the label for products that exfoliate with the benefit of ground-up nutshells and other all-natural ingredients.

GO EASY ON THE 'POO. Shampoos, conditioners, soaps, moisturizing lotions, and sunscreens contain complex chemicals that can evade conventional sewage treatment and end up flowing into rivers and oceans. Use less of your usual brand or opt for all-natural formulations.

GET YOUR LAWN OFF CHEMICALS. Acre for acre, homeowners apply much more chemical fertilizers, herbicides, and pesticides to lawns and gardens than farmers lay down on their fields. Switch to organic gardening and lawn maintenance instead, but even natural fertilizers and weed preventers must be applied carefully to avoid runoff.

FIX YOUR OIL SPILL. Oil leaking from your car's engine contributes to an annual flow of pollution equal in size to the *Exxon Valdez* oil spill. If you've sprung a leak, see your mechanic, pronto.

PICK UP AFTER YOUR POOCH. They may be cute, but your pets deposit excrement that's high in nutrients, bacteria, and other stuff that can cause algae blooms and disease once it enters a body of water. Scoop up the poop and put it in a paper sack before disposing.

THE TASMAN SEA IN AUTUMN BROUGHT SOME OF THE MOST
BEAUTIFUL, AS WELL AS ROUGHEST, SAILING.

into perspective. I've tried different cameras, lenses, angles, f-stops, shutters, but I'm not really able to capture the same image and feeling I get being here. There's something poetic in that.

Then there's that other 10 percent of waves. During daylight hours, you can usually tell if a wave is going to crash about three seconds before it does. You have some responsibilities to fulfill within those three seconds. First, you yell, "Wave!" to warn those inside to brace for impact. Second, you grab ahold of the helm and brace your feet in an aggressively wide stance. Third, you cover and, quite naturally, pray, and hold your breath simultaneously. It feels like a three-story apartment building made of water has fallen on your back. All better. You look up and recover. You're alive. You yell or laugh something at having accepted Mother Nature's biggest bear hug.

..........................

With unfailing accuracy, the "track" function on our marine GPS system let us see our sailing course displayed as a thin red line superimposed on nautical charts. In the days following the big blow that almost took down our mast, our sailing track looked less like purposeful progression toward Australia than a squirrel's hunt for a half-remembered buried nut. We circled, doglegged, jagged, and went every which way but the direction we intended: southwest. On July 17, we drifted into Australian waters. Just 200 miles to go, but with no wind it might as well have been a thousand. We sat in mirror-flat water, slowly being pushed northward by unseen currents.

In twenty-four hours, the first of two storm fronts of Antarctic origin barreling up the Tasman Sea was forecast to hit. Each storm promised to shove us farther north toward the dangerous reefs and shoals of the Coral Sea. We were sitting ducks.

I had a solution. "Jo, since no matter where we land we're going to need a tow down the coast, and we're due in Sydney on the twenty-fifth for all those welcoming festivities, why not arrange for a tow in from here?"

Jo took to the idea immediately and got on the satellite phone to inquire about available towing. The prices some boat owners quoted amounted to high-seas robbery. I got on the phone to try my luck. With each dead end I reached, the *Plastiki* crew grew antsier. Four months at sea on our small boat was taking its toll. Max was after Jo every twenty minutes with the same questions: "Are we there? When are we getting there? Jo, what's going on?"

From a list of possible towing options supplied by our ever-capable shore crew of Adventure Ecology staff based in Sydney, I made contact with the Australian Volunteer Coast Guard in Mooloolaba. By all means, they said. It'll be a total honor. We can be there in twelve to fifteen hours. At $150 an hour, the price was right, and the deal was struck.

"David. David. You need to wake up." Jo was gently tapping my shoulder. "The Coast Guard has put out a statement that they've come to rescue us. The media has picked up on it."

"Oh, damn. That's the last thing we need." And by the way, why do all the crises around here have to happen during the few hours I'm ever asleep?

As it turned out, the local coast guard had indeed commented to the media, claiming that a rescue was in the works. Faster than you can say "Colorado balloon-boy hoax," sailing-oriented Web sites and Australian media had seized on the news. PLASTIKI AVOIDS STICKY SITUATION and PLASTIKI SENDS OUT PAN PAN, RESCUE UNDERWAY, blared headlines. "Water police based in Brisbane have picked up a distress call from *Plastiki*, the eco-friendly 60-ft. catamaran made of 12,000 plastic bottles. *Plastiki* was 200 nautical miles off the coast, her engine was disabled, and she was being driven helplessly north by strong trade winds. 'It's the furtherest [sic] we have

THE SIGHT OF A SEAGULL LET THE CREW KNOW
THAT AUSTRALIAN LAND WAS NOT FAR AWAY.

LAND HO! REACHING THE COAST OF AUSTRALIA WAS A STEP AWAY FROM SYDNEY BUT FELT LIKE AN END FOR *PLASTIKI*'S LONG ADVENTURE.

ever had to go for a rescue operation, and we were the only ones who could do it,' said the commander," read one article.

What? Rescue? Engine failure? Distress call? We'd survived storms of every description while sailing 8,000 miles, and now *Plastiki*'s message of hope was in danger of being diluted by a media firestorm. How did our simple business arrangement get so twisted around? All I can conclude is fee-for-tow isn't part of the Volunteer Coast Guard's charter, and the commander was covering his ass.

We had to nip this in the bud. Adventure Ecology's crack media team in London soon issued a statement setting the record straight—which the media did its best to ignore. Rather than fully savor the giant accomplishment of making it to Australia, I instead spent most of the next two days on the phone with reporters for TV and radio stations, newspapers, wire services, magazines, and Web sites from around the world getting our side of the story out about the rescue that wasn't. Oh well, in PR circles they say any news is good news.

In the end, the local coast guard unit did tow us into Mooloolaba, we did make a "contribution" to the Australian Volunteer Coast Guard, and at the sight of Australia's deep yellow beaches I did practically weep. "That's Australia," I told myself. "That. Is. Australia. We made it!"

I'd been scrupulously taking every day as it came, not thinking about an endpoint, and now Australia, for so long just an abstract point on the map, was in front of me. Four years of dreaming big, tossing about ideas, building, innovating, and sailing had led us to this odd place, Mooloolaba, 470 miles north of Sydney.

As we neared the harbor at Mooloolaba, a helicopter buzzed overhead. People lined the seawall, their cell phones and digital cameras at arm's length, snapping photos of the curious bottle-boat in their midst. Still more spectators were streaming in from all points. Reporters waited on the dock, their microphones at the ready. Before any of us could disembark to take a first step on Australian soil, a team of customs officials rushed aboard. They had a field day confiscating all of the raw and sprouting foods contained in our cupboards. One official dashed out holding a sack of beans as though it were radioactive. Mr. T, never a big veggie lover, was grinning. "Thank God we're getting rid of that stuff," he said.

Finally ashore, we were swallowed by the crowd. The energy was amazing. Handshakes, backslaps, and questions rained down on us. "You've come all the way from San Francisco?" I heard over and again. A gentleman approached with a gift. A kangaroo-skin hat. "If you're going to be in Australia, you have to wear an Akubra," he said, handing it to me.

We still had to get to Sydney, where media events, speeches, and fanfare awaited, but our arrival here in Mooloolaba felt like an ending. No more nights sitting out under picture-book constellations, watching for shooting stars and swirling phosphorescence. No more of that last-people-on-earth intimacy with Jo, Mr. T, Vern, Max, Matt, Graham, Luca, and Singeli. The purity and intensity of the voyage was past. But *Plastiki*'s affirming message that we can solve the problem of plastics in the oceans through ingenuity had only just started.

*Plastiki* had succeeded in reaching a global audience beyond any of our wildest imaginings. Our safe arrival in the land of Oz brought an outpouring of good wishes from *Plastiki*'s legions of fans and friends following our adventure on Facebook, Twitter, YouTube, and Flickr. Through thousands of news reports, *Plastiki* had slipped into the global zeitgeist and played no small part in bringing intense media and institutional focus to the plight of our oceans and the need for immediate action to save them. Those issues can seem daunting, but I'd like to think that *Plastiki* proved, if nothing else, that when you follow an audacious dream into the unknown, the journey itself can be inspiring in ways beyond imagining.

## EPILOGUE

PLASTIKI'S ENTRANCE INTO SYDNEY HARBOR WAS THE BEGINNING OF AN EVEN GREATER ADVENTURE: CHANGING HOW WE TREAT WASTE AND HOW WE TREAT OUR PLANET.

ON JULY 26, PLASTIKI TRIUMPHANTLY SAILED OR,
MORE ACCURATELY, WAS TOWED INTO SYDNEY HARBOR. AS A TEAM,
WE HAD SPENT MORE THAN 120 DAYS ON AN EXPEDITION WHOSE MISSION
WAS TO BEAT WASTE BY SHOWCASING SOLUTIONS IN A WAY THAT WOULD
CAPTURE THE IMAGINATION AND STIR ACTION.

With passion, curiosity, and sheer determination, we took a crazy idea and made it a reality.

At the time of our arrival in the harbor, I stood excitedly at the stern of *Plastiki* watching the welcoming party of boats frantically zipping past while news helicopters hovered above like birds of prey. I clearly remember trying hard to keep my composure, to control my emotions as a cocktail of excitement and nerves coursed through my body, driving me to the point of distraction around what we had all just achieved. We had made it! San Francisco to Sydney on a boat made out of bottles. We had really done it. No one could take that away from us!

I would be lying if I said I wasn't feeling a little smug at that point toward all those who doubted and tried to crush the dream. We had overcome huge and numerous obstacles to create the adventure that delivered the message in a way that I couldn't ever have imagined all those years ago!

Now, post-expedition and back in Los Angeles, I'm surrounded by the sound of cars, not boats, zipping past;

police sirens, not media helicopters, flying above; and I'm starting to feel the bittersweetness that comes in the wake of any expedition. The salt long washed from my body, *Plastiki*'s movement dissolved from my legs, and the privilege of calling the ocean my home is no longer mine. In exchange for my moment deep in nature, where every day was simple and complete, I have returned to a world full of small details, to lists of chores, and human causes and effects.

The sterility of being surrounded by what on the surface feels like a purely human world makes the past months of my life feel like a distant fantasy, albeit a very rich and humbling one. As I stand at the checkout of Bed Bath & Beyond—and my has it gone beyond!—I can't but help notice that for all of Team *Plastiki*'s efforts, our voracious appetite for and addiction to one-time-use plastics are far from abating. In fact, in contrast to the sparseness of the ocean, it feels even more plastic.

Back on dry land, my breath seems shorter and faster. Things seem to skim, blip, pop, and pulse quicker,

*PLASTIKI* FINDS PROTECTED WATERS AND A MOMENT OF CALM WHILE ROUNDING MIDDLE HEAD ON THE APPROACH TO SYDNEY HARBOR.

SMILE FOR THE CAMERAS! THE TRIUMPHANT CREW JUST BEFORE DOCKING AT CIRCULAR QUAY AT THE HEART OF SYDNEY.

and it's exactly this everyday pulse that is so distracting, making it seemingly impossible to comprehend the ever-growing and devastating set of plastic fingerprints on our natural world. Rather than feel depressed or despondent about the situation, I feel oddly more driven and more compelled than ever to take my anything-is-possible feeling and apply it toward loosening our stranglehold on natural environments.

I am now more driven to start, arguably, the most important and critical chapter in *Plastiki*'s mission to beat waste: a chapter of Change! Change that can dramatically shift our daily habits away from an unnecessary and destructive addiction to single-use plastics, but even more important and urgent, a change in attitudes toward understanding, valuing, and protecting one of our planet's most precious and important natural systems: our oceans.

No longer is it acceptable to continue just articulating our Planet 1.0 failures. We now must all show leadership and vision to support the stories, individuals, and initiatives that help us to dream bigger, undertake more compelling adventures, and fundamentally inspire, motivate, and innovate solutions.

Our failure to achieve such an outcome will undoubtedly leave humanity's ability to live on this planet as we know it in the balance. The time to give ourselves a chance of survival is truly upon us. To create the radical shift that's required in our current system and the stories that we tell ourselves, each and every one of us must now try to dig deep and find our own *Plastiki*—to act now! I know I am.

AFTER 8,000 MILES OF NEAR-ISOLATION, DAVID DE ROTHSCHILD GREETS A SWARM OF REPORTERS AND PHOTOGRAPHERS AFTER STEPPING ASHORE IN SYDNEY.

CLOCKWISE FROM TOP LEFT: DAVID GREETS A WELL-WISHER; VERN REUNITES WITH HIS THREE-MONTH-OLD SON; DAVID FIELDS THE FIRST OF MANY QUESTIONS; DAVID, JO, AND MATT CHEER FULFILLING A DREAM.

# ACKNOWLEDGMENTS

**CREW**
Singeli Agnew
Luca Babini
Matthew Grey
Olav Heyerdahl
Graham Hill
Max Jourdan
Vern Moen
Jo Royle
David Thomson

**TEAM**
Katie Ardern
Charlotte Bufton
Tia Grazette
Mark Headley
Gail Devlin Jones
Annabel Lander
Martin Metz
Ben Murtagh
Charlie O'Malley
Rebecca Petzel
Chris Sills
Satpal Singh
Jamie Strecker
Katie Tilleke
Emma Voller
Kevin Williams
Ron Yoon

**BUILD & DEVELOPMENT**
Ashley Biggin — Boat Builder
Nathaniel Corum — Architecture for Humanity
Liz Diaz — North Beach Marine Canvas
Rick Didia — Shipwright
Tommy Dixon — Shipwright
Andy Dovell — Naval Architect
Andy Fox — Boat Builder
George — Coast Marine
Nick Hewlings — Shipwright
Jason and Camilla Iftakhar — Jamily Design Studio
Kelly — Shipwright
Liz and Ian at DOER
Gordy Nash — Boat Builder
Mike O'Reilly — Smarter Planet, Inc.
Michael Pawlyn — Exploration Architecture
Greg Pronko— Smarter Planet, Inc.
Dave Pryce —Shipwright
Mike Rose — Boat Builder
Peter Rubin — Iron Rooster Studios
Elena Sanchez, Monico Corall — Port of San Francisco

Zac, Edwin, Carlos, Marcos, Louis, Angel, Daire, Montse, Stefan, Sarah, Mike "the light," Eva, Rutso, Rick and Ed — Professional Finishers Richmond

**OPERATIONS & LOGISTICS**
Buzz Ballenger — Ballenger Spars
Reason Bradley — Inertia Labs
Ray Deiter — Sea Trials Support
Paul Dines — SF Bay Adventures
Ed Dunn — HANC Recycling
Josh Hall — Safety Manager
Rebecca Jewell — Waste Management
Paul Kaplan — KKMI
Richard Lauer — AMCOR PET
Minta Burn, Kim McKay — Momentum 2
Rob Mazza — Alcan Baltek
Joe Pantalone — Alcan Baltek
Sturge Taylor — Insurers
Neil Thomas — Atelier 1 Engineers
Mark Thompson — Expedition Doctor
Tony Varni — 7UP Bottling Co — bottle caps
Mark Weisz — CS Marine Cranes
Under Writing Risk Services — Insurers

**PARTNERS**
HP — Technology Partner
Inmarsat — Global Satellite Communications Provider
IWC Schaffhausen— Official Partner
Kiehl's — Expedition Supplier (cosmetics and toiletries)
Revo — Sunglasses Provider

**INDIVIDUALS**
Patrick Baker
Jon Bowermaster
Tony Chapman
Karina Deyko
Brett Ellsworth
Anthony de Rothschild
Evelyn de Rothschild
Jessica de Rothschild
Loki de Rothschild
Lou Lou de Rothschild
Mia de Rothschild
Tania de Rothschild
Lady Victoria de Rothschild
Graham Dodd
Peter Drake
David Enthoven
Kit Hawkins
Karta Healy
Josian Heyerdahl
Jay Little

Chris Luebkeman
Mayor Gavin Newsom
Hem Patel
Susan Reeve
Trevor Rowe
Renne Robeson
Peter Robeson
Lewis Schott
Nash Schott
Aniko Schott
Steve Schott
Neil Thomas
John Trevillian

## NETWORK
The Algalita Research Foundation
ARUP
The Australian National Maritime Museum
Circle of Blue
Clean Up the World
CNN International
The Collective
Creme de La Mer
The Design Museum London
The Fish Film Company
Global Green
Global Oceans
Glodownead Communications
Grades of Green
The Green Initiative
Kon-Tiki Museum
Long Beach Film Company
Momentum 2
NASA
National Geographic
Nickelodeon
Nike
NOAA
Oceanic Preservation Society
Oprah Winfrey and the Oprah.com team
Plastic Pollution Coalition
The Prince's Rainforest Project
Project Kaisei
Renegade
The Royal Geographical Society
Scripps Institute of Oceanography
Surf Rider Foundation
Sydney Institute of Marine Science
Tom's Shoes
Treehugger.com
UNEP
University of California, San Diego
University of San Francisco
University of Sydney
The Virgin Group
World Watch Institute
Youth Noise

## OPINION PIECE CONTRIBUTORS
Susan Casey
Celine Cousteau

Philippe Cousteau
Sylvia Earle
Marcus Eriksen
Angelina Jolie
Sir Ian Kiernan
William McDonough
Captain Charles Moore
Bruce Parry
Louie Psihoyos
Parrys Raines
Dr. Enric Sala
Dr. Greg Stone
Robin Williams
Doug Woodring

## SUPPORTERS
Ampair — wind turbines
Australian National Maritime Museum
Australian Volunteer Coast Guard Mooloolaba
Roger Badham — Weather Routing
Ian Black — Transam Samoa
John Brydon — JMB Kiribati
Darling Harbour Water Police
DB Shenker Australia
Dimension-Polyant — sail cloth technology
Eagle Claw — fishing tackle
Andrew Copely — Skipper JBW
Gill — sailing clothing
Bill Goggins and Don Whelan, Harken —
sailing hardware for boat
Joe Haller and Ian Hannula, Nice Collective — clothing
and interiors design, manufacture and fitting
Mike Higgins, Human Dynamo — on-board bike
Inka Biospheric Systems — producers and installers of the hydroponic garden
IQ Solar — solar panel manufacturers
Jeppensen Marine
Klean Kanteen — aluminum bottles as replacements
for water bottles
Sean Langman — Noakes Boat Yard
Leica — camera equipment provider
Malcolm Morgan, Morgan Designs, Inc. — marine electrical company
Mirvac — accommodations in Sydney
Mountain Equipment — clothing
Nature Valley — food provider
PNY — designer and manufacturer of memory upgrade products
Remote Satellite Systems — satellite communication technologies
Kame Richards, Pineapple Sails — cloth sails
Sapa — mast
Rick Sheema — Weather Routing
Shortomatic — board shorts designed and provided for the Plastiki crew
Sky Eye — Weather, Tracking, and Communications
Luis Soltero, Global Marine Network — satellite
communication system
Eric Steinberg, Farralon Electronics
Jennifer Tuck and Nona Lim — sourced, cooked, and packed food
Students of UCLA Architecture
Seth Wachtel and students, University of San Francisco
Scott Wallace — Billabong
John Winning — Owner JBW
Steve Zavestowski and students, University of San Francisco

Produced by

MELCHER
MEDIA

124 West 13th Street
New York, NY 10011
www.melcher.com

**President and Publisher:** Charles Melcher
**Associate Publisher:** Bonnie Eldon
**Editor in Chief:** Duncan Bock
**Executive Editor:** Lia Ronnen
**Production Director:** Kurt Andrews

**Editor:** David E. Brown
**Production Coordinator:** Daniel del Valle

**Designer:** Ben Gibson
**Design Advisor:** Tia Grazette

Melcher Media would also like to thank Max Dickstein, Jim Gorman, Parlan McGaw, Lauren Nathan, Holly Rothman, Larry Schwartz, Julia Sourikoff, Shoshana Thaler, and Megan Worman.

FSC
www.fsc.org
MIX
Paper from
responsible sources
FSC® C008047

**CREDITS**

**Illustrations by Jon Vermilyea**

**Courtesy of Plastiki:** 2-3, 71, 102–103, 132–33 (all), 138–39, 148 (top), 210–11 (all), 217 (top right)
**Luca Babini, courtesy of Plastiki:** 10–11, 26, 30–31, 32–33, 33 (inset), 34–35, 47, 48, 55, 68–69 (all), 76, 122, 134–35, 142, 145, 146 (bottom right), 156–57, 159, 161 (all). 166–67, 170, 172–73, 176–77, 193, 202 (all), 207 (all), 208, 213, 217 (bottom right, bottom left), 224, 232–33
**David de Rothschild, courtesy of Plastiki:** 6–7, 9, 72–73, 75, 79, 80 (all), 81 (all), 110–11, 113, 114 (bottom), 117, 120, 121, 124–25 (all), 146 (top left, top right, bottom left), 148 (bottom), 152–53, 180–81, 192, 198–99, 201, 204–205, 220–21, 223, back cover (top right)
**Matthew Grey, courtesy of Plastiki:** 29, 38–39, 42 (all), 44, 46, 52, 54, 58–59, 62–63, 65, 141, 149 (all), 217 (top left)
**Olav Heyerdahl, courtesy of Plastiki:** 119
**Vern Moen, courtesy of Plastiki:** 13, 67, 114 (top, middle), 115, 130–31, back cover (left)
**Andrew Rae, courtesy of Plastiki:** 56–57

**Courtesy of Algalita Marine Research Foundation:** 104
**Benjamin Allder/Aventure Ecology:** 92–93, 95
**Getty Images/AFP:** 185 (left)
**Getty Images/Laurent Fievet:** 185 (right)
**Martin Hartley:** 14–15
**© Sophie Henson:** 89
**© Lindsey Hoshaw:** 16, 90, 98 (top right, bottom right, bottom left), 107
**Kon-Tiki Museum:** 20
**Courtesy of McGilvra Elementary School:** 162 (all)
**Jean-Paul Ferrero/Auscape/Minden Pictures:** 163
**Courtesy of Michael Pawlyn:** 23, 24 (all), 41
**© Photolibrary:** 86–87, 100–101, 183, 190–91
**© Brittany M. Powell:** 106
**Patrick Riviere:** Cover, 226–27, 229, 230–31, 234 (all), 235 (all), back cover (bottom right)
**Courtesy of Mike Rose:** 50 (all)
**J. Leichter/© 2009 Scripps Institution of Oceanography:** 98 (top left)

**Monterey Bay Aquarium Seafood Watch guidelines courtesy of Monterey Bay Aquarium**

*With special thanks to the Plastiki's partners and sponsors*